Black Sea

Bithynia & Pontus

Mysia

Galatia

Cappadocia

Asia

Ephesus

Colossae

Tarsus

Syria

Antioch

Cyprus

Damascus

rete

ean Sea

Jerusalem

Egypt

PAUL OF TARSUS

PAUL OF TARSUS

A VISIONARY LIFE

Edward Stourton

HiddenSpring

Published in Great Britain by Hodder & Stoughton
A Division of Hodder Headline Ltd, 338 Euston Road, London, NW1 3BH
www.madaboutbooks.com

Library of Congress Cataloging-in-Publication Data

Stourton, Edward.
Paul of Tarsus : a visionary life / Edward Stourton.
p. cm.
Includes bibliographical references and index.
ISBN 1-58768-032-7 (cloth : alk. paper)
1. Paul, the Apostle, Saint. 2. Christian saints—Turkey—Tarsus—Biography.
3. Apostles—Biography. 4. Tarsus (Turkey)—Biography. 5. Paul, the Apostle,
Saint—Travel—Mediterranean Region. 6. Mediterranean Region—Description
and travel. I. Title.
BS2506.3.S76 2005
225.9'2—dc22

2005009230

Published in the United States in 2005 by

HiddenSpring
An imprint of Paulist Press
997 Macarthur Boulevard
Mahwah, New Jersey 07430

www.hiddenspringbooks.com

Printed and bound in the
United States of America

Contents

Acknowledgments

I owe my thanks above all to Phil Pegum, the BBC producer who, in an appropriately Damascene flash of inspiration in a church in Cyprus, dreamt up the idea of a Radio Four series that would follow St. Paul around the old Roman world. David Coomes and Helen Boaden at Radio Four gave the idea their blessing, and Phil and I made our journey in the apostle's footsteps together. Many of the ideas that underlie this book are his, and he has been unfailingly generous with his time and his expertise. I feel more than a little guilty that my name rather than his is on the cover of this book.

My agent Vivienne Schuster has been a wonderfully energizing source of encouragement, and I am very grateful to my editor, Judith Longman, for the gentle but rigorous way in which she has helped me to discipline the text (which sometimes showed a tendency to take off in unlikely directions that surprised even me), and her patience with a project that took rather longer than it should have. The staff at the London Library deserve infinite praise for making it such an appealing place to work that I found myself actively looking forward to my days researching there, and my wife Fiona read and improved every chapter—as well as enduring my black moods over a task that I sometimes felt was beyond me.

Finally I owe a debt to all those who guided me on my journey. St. Paul seems to make people want to talk about him, and almost everyone I met—academics, priests, tour guides, and pilgrims—was ready to offer me the intellectual equivalent of open house.

Introduction

The Apostle to the Gentiles is, at first glance, an unlikely twenty-first-century hero. The charges laid against him—that he is homophobic, bigoted about women, and anti-Semitic—are cardinal sins of today's culture. He was irredeemably irascible—even scholars who have lavished a lifetime on his writings say they would find him impossible company at dinner—and he stirred up strife wherever he went. He sometimes took a view of tolerance that would make a Taliban blush; we are told, for example, that in his preconversion role as an officially approved persecutor of Christians he turned out to watch the stoning of Stephen with some enthusiasm. And I suspect that almost anyone who had a conventional Christian upbringing would share the view I formed of him as a child: that he is a dry old stick whose writings were always being used by the grown-ups to forbid us from doing things that sounded like fun.

But the better I came to know Paul, the less secure I felt in my prejudices. He is an elusive figure (partly because of his infuriating contradictions), but every so often, I felt I caught a glimpse of him, chatting up Lydia by the stream in Philippi or striding up and down a room overlooking the sea at Ephesus, pouring out words so fast that his scribe cannot keep up. Paul was anything but dry. In fact, if he had a fault, it lay in the opposite direction, in an excess of passion. And his passion makes him a compelling and engaging figure.

I am by no means the first to find myself becoming steadily more "hooked" on Paul as I have learned more about him. When the German theologian Adolf Deissmann set out in the apostle's footsteps in 1906, he described his objective like this: "to come back from the paper Paul of our western libraries, from the Germanized, dogmatized, modernized, stilted Paul, to the historic Paul, through the labyrinth of 'Paulinism,' of the New Testament theology, to gain contact once again with the actual Paul of ancient days." He concluded his journey with a mixture of affection and frustration I find all too familiar: "There has probably seldom been," Deissmann declared, "anyone at the same time hated with such fiery hatred and loved with such strong passion as Paul."

Paul's letters are—and it is impossible to ignore the importance of this once you have thought about it for a moment or two—the earliest Christian documents we have. They give us vivid, firsthand testimony, and bring him alive in a way the gospels can never do for Christ. If you put them together with the detailed—if sometimes questionable—biography of Paul provided by the Acts of the Apostles, you can anchor him in place and history with a focus you cannot quite find when you follow the Jesus story.

There really is an amphitheater in Ephesus where the silversmiths rioted because they feared that Paul threatened their trade in pagan effigies, and I bumped into a group of American tourists there reading aloud from the story in Acts. The city of Corinth— to which Paul sent his stern injunctions on sexual morality—was such a cesspit of lewdness that "to Corinth" meant "having sex" in the ancient world. And there is to this day a "street called Straight" cutting through the heart of the old city in Damascus— every bit as busy and noisy as one imagines it to have been when Ananias was sent down it to find Paul after his Damascene conversion. The building known as Ananias's house is looked after by a Franciscan friar called Brother Tom; the Chicago drawl and the piece of licorice lodged permanently in his cheek make him difficult to decipher, but he dismisses other places of pilgrimage—like Bethlehem—in near verbless staccato: "This is it," as he looks around his tiny, numinous compound, "this is unique, St. Paul— great saint."

After spending several months in Paul's company, I have come to suspect that part of the fascination he exercises is akin to the passion for genealogy that seems to be driving people in their

Introduction

millions to trawl the Internet for information about their ancestors. Paul is the intellectual forebear of anyone who was brought
up in the framework of once Christian Europe. He is one of a
handful of towering figures who formed our way of thinking, and
when you read his letters you are going back to your roots. You
may not always like what you find—just as it can be a bit unsettling to discover that great-great-uncle Harry was hanged for
sheep stealing—but you cannot get away from the fact that you
have inherited his intellectual genes.

And far from slipping over the horizon of history, Paul is
lurking behind many of today's headlines. I made my Pauline pilgrimage in the aftermath of the terrorist attacks of September 11,
2001, and when I was not wending my way through the ancient
streets of Corinth or Philippi, I was covering the news in
Washington, D.C., or Kabul, New York or Peshawar. Paul's
legacy, I soon realized, was just as much at the center of the stage
in the great contemporary drama I was witnessing as he himself
was in the drama of the Acts of the Apostles.

He is responsible for the biggest bone of contention
between Christianity and Islam—the fault line, in fact, which so
many people have been struggling to understand since September
11. Islam holds that the one true religion was taught to
humankind through a series of prophets, each of whom brought
a revealed book—the Torah from Moses, for example, the Psalms
from David, and the Gospels from Jesus. Muhammad was the last
and greatest of the prophets, but Jesus still holds an important
place in Islamic teaching.

The division between the two faiths arises above all over the
issue of Christ's divinity, which for Islam distorts the purity of
monotheism. And Paul, the passionate proselytizer of Christ as
the path to salvation, is identified as the figure who "turned Jesus
into a god." Because Paul's letters predate the gospels it is very
easy to argue that the gospel account of Jesus' life is written to
match his ideas. Zaki Badawi of the Muslim College in London
describes Paul as "the principle obstacle to greater harmony
between Christians and Muslims."

Badawi also subscribes to the theory—increasingly popular,
especially among the apostle's many enemies—that Paul, not

3

Christ, is the true founder of Christianity. There is a strong case that Christianity began as an argument among Jews—specifically as an argument between St. Peter and St. Paul about that most Jewish of rites, circumcision. Peter was of the "circumcision party," those who held that to become a follower of Christ a Gentile must be circumcised and follow Jewish Law. Paul believed that Christ was a liberation from the Law, and, as he famously put it, that "a person is justified not by the works of the law but through faith in Jesus Christ" (Gal 2:16). Paul won the argument, and that was the moment when the followers of Christ became distinct from the other Jewish sects knocking around in mid-first-century Jerusalem. God's chosen people now meant all humankind, and the foundations for a worldwide religion were laid.

Understanding Paul's part in the process made me feel queasy. He never met Christ before his crucifixion and there is almost nothing in his letters about Jesus' earlier life and teachings; yet it is possible to argue that he effectively founded the Christian church by defying the apostle whom Christ had chosen as "the rock on whom I will build my church." Suddenly the Christ of the gospels seemed a less certain figure.

Paul's argument with Peter explains why he is every bit as controversial a figure among Jews as he is among Muslims. It may have been settled within the church, but in today's Israel the question behind it is anything but; should Judaism look inward and live only in its history, or should it turn its face towards the wider world and the rest of humankind? It is a question that always hovers in the background of the prolonged agony that is the Middle East crisis.

The way Paul resolved it has led to perhaps the gravest charge of all those laid at his door—that, Jew though he was, he is the father of anti-Semitism. Daniel Schwartz, Professor of Jewish History at the Hebrew University in Jerusalem, accuses him of "polemics against Judaism." In Paul's writing, he says, "the way of Jesus is over the way of Moses, there's this way and there's that way, and they are much more separate from one another than they were in the teaching of Jesus himself."

Introduction

I discussed Paul with two religious writers in Jerusalem—Yossi Klein Halevi of *Jerusalem Report* and Rabbi David Rosen, the international director of inter-religious relations at the American Jewish Committee, and was astonished by the rawness of the feelings he still stirs up. Even today most Jews, says Rabbi Rosen, "don't have the emotional or psychological capacity to look with a degree of objectivity" at Paul. That is perhaps not altogether surprising in view of the baggage that history has dumped on the way he is remembered—the Diaspora and the Holocaust are bound to color the way Jews look at him. But it sill came as a shock to be told that "names that are at the very heart of the Christian faith are perceived by the vast majority of Jews as symbols of the historical dehumanization and demonization of the Jewish people."

Yossi Klein Halevi blames Paul for taking what was essentially a family quarrel within Judaism and exposing it to the world and to history. Jews, he suggests, can be as rude as they want to each other as long as they keep their arguments to themselves. "When you go to the Hebrew prophets and you look at some of the ways they talk, you could almost perceive it as anti-Semitic," he says, comparing it to the vigorous language of debate in contemporary Israeli politics. "Paul is the one who takes this internal conflict and allows the rest of the world to eavesdrop on it."

Rabbi Rosen believes Jews will be able to look at Paul more steadily as they "become more secure in the world"—we were speaking just before a suicide bomber devastated a street in downtown Jerusalem not far from his office. But Paul would have been instinctively at home with both the political and religious debates in today's Israel. He was disputatious by nature, never more himself than when causing some kind of affray because of his ideas.

At more or less every stop I made on my journey in his footsteps, I found Paul a source of sharp insight into the politics and religion of today's Middle East and southern Europe. And I especially valued his company in the corridors of the Vatican.

The Vatican's chief Latinist—an immensely engaging enthusiast who had translated the instructions on the Vatican cash machines into the language of the Romans—complained to me that there was not much "coming down the hall" these days.

There was a time when the fertile mind of John Paul II kept Father Reg and his team up late at nights—struggling to fit the capacious and free-ranging ideas of the philosopher pope into the straitjacket of what is still the church's official means of communication. But by the time of our meeting the stream of encyclicals had dried up, and there was a feeling of ossification in the offices and courtyards around St. Peter's; the old pope's astonishing intellectual fertility was failing, and his officials were busily tidying up his inspirations and turning his ideas into laws.

Paul of course would be horrified by that. "Christ has set us free," he wrote, "do not submit again to a yoke of slavery" (Gal 5:1). The idea that religion lies in your head and in your heart and not in a set of regulations is so familiar to us that we seldom pause to reflect on it, but it was perhaps Paul's greatest contribution to the history of thought.

Standing at the entrance to the theater in Ephesus, looking down the avenue of gracious columns that once led to the sea, I was struck by what a thrill it must have been to hear that message for the first time. Paul was preaching to the subjects of an empire that in material terms had a sophistication that we still marvel at today. Yet its religions were mixed and messy—surely too crude and confused for the people who created these extraordinary cities.

Paul would be astonished by the way his letters are used in the church today. Apart from anything else, he believed the Second Coming would happen in his lifetime, so he certainly was not writing for posterity. And it is difficult to believe that he would approve of the Sacred Congregation for the Doctrine of the Faith, the body that codifies the orthodoxy of the Catholic Church.

Most of his letters were written to deal with specific practical problems that cropped up in the churches he had founded around the Roman world—whether it was the Corinthians giving in to the general randiness of their city or St. Peter backsliding on the question of circumcision. That means their theology is much more closely based in day-to-day experience than the "top-down" method of establishing moral norms favored in the modern Vatican.

Introduction

If Paul were around today he would not be sitting in Rome thinking—he would be out in the world developing practical theology. It is of course impossible to say quite what he would have made of something like the church's teaching on contraception in the face of the AIDS crisis in Africa—to take an especially difficult example of Catholicism's dilemmas—but I am sure you would find him in the townships of South Africa or the compounds around Lusaka trying to work through his theology with the benefit of firsthand experience. The tone of his letters suggests he would do it in the manner of the modern intellectual, not the traditional theologian; he is a restless thinker, constantly agonizing and driving his ideas up experimental alleyways that sometimes turn out to lead nowhere. He searches for truth with his imagination as much as his reason, and his writing is full of paradox and passion.

Although he never wavers in the certainty of faith in the risen Christ, neither is he frightened of exploring fully the complexity of an argument. Finally (and this I found especially appealing), stern moralist though he may be, he often seems to find it difficult to condemn anyone outright; his letters are full of warmth and affection toward his friends.

The novelist A. N. Wilson, who has written a biography of Paul, has come to a truly subversive conclusion about the Apostle to the Gentiles. Paul's Christianity, he says, "is a whole new way of looking at the world, not a set or rules...he would have thought most forms of institutional Christianity were fleshly, were carnal, were diabolical, basically."

It makes him sound like a very twenty-first-century prophet of New Age religion. Walking across St. Peter's Square, gazing up at the basilica, I felt rather guilty about allowing such a thought to cross my mind.

I stopped for a moment between the two monumental statues that welcome you up the steps to the church: St. Peter, with his keys to the kingdom of heaven on one side, St. Paul, with his sword of truth on the other. The way they are placed is supposed to reflect their joint contribution to the Christian faith. If I think back over my own experience of Catholicism, I would have to admit that Peter has been a much more prominent presence. He is, after all, the basis for the papal claim to primacy, while Paul committed the unforgivable sin of being a hero for Martin Luther and the Reformation. But no amount of rummaging through history can make Peter the kind of vital and engaging figure I found Paul to be, and I could not help feeling a Protestant Pauline tug at my Catholic roots.

This project began as a straightforward physical journey in the steps of the apostle across the old Roman world. But at each stop I found myself drawn down one of the many avenues of influence that lead from St. Paul's life to the present day, and this became a journey of intellectual exploration.

1

A Child of His Time

To find the cave you climb westward up the hill with your back to the Temple of Domitian, leaving the private houses behind on your right. The path disappears into the scrub from time to time, twisting back on itself when you find it again, as you rise above the city. After ten minutes' stiff walking you pause to catch your breath, and from here the big landmarks stand out below you—the theater carved out of the hill on the other side of the valley, the Marble Street, and in the distance the Arcadian Way. In St. Paul's time the colonnades of this chic shopping arcade (this was one of only three cities in the Roman Empire to enjoy the benefits of street lighting) led down to the harbor, but the Mediterranean has long since retreated, and Ephesus is now marooned in the Turkish landscape.

The entrance to the cave is half hidden by a fold in the hill. It has been given a stone façade, so that it looks like a small chapel. There are so many glories of past greatness at Ephesus that it is perhaps unsurprising that it attracted little notice for so long. The first modern record we have of its existence is dated 1905, and for most of the twentieth century it seems have been co-opted by the local shepherds as a suitable spot for kebab cooking while on duty.

In 1995 the entrance was rediscovered by the Austrian archaeologist Renata Pillinger, and inside she found plasterwork covered with Christian graffiti. Together with Dr. Ruth Ohm, the curator of the Baden Institute of Biblical Archaeology at Berkley, California, and with the support of a single local assistant, she rigged up a system of mirrors that would provide enough light to work on the find. They transcribed hundreds of pieces of graffiti

9

with painstaking care, and it proved a scholarly treasure trove. The graffiti were written over a period of several centuries—from the fifth century until the 1920s—and Paul's name keeps cropping up; the cave had evidently been some kind of shrine to the apostle.

But in the best archaeological tradition—and Ruth Ohm's voice still trembles with excitement when she describes this—the most significant discovery came about by accident. During a break in the work Renata Pillinger was scratching at some of the loose plaster at the back of the cave with her fingernails, and she caught a glimpse of colors beneath. Under the plaster the team found an extraordinary and luminous sequence of paintings; monumental images of the twelve apostles surround the back section of the cave, and nearer the front, on the right as you enter, there is a vivid and arresting picture of St. Paul. He has short hair and a grizzled black beard. One hand is raised—whether in blessing or admonition it is difficult to tell—and he gazes out at you with piercing eyes, Ancient Mariner-like in the way he commands attention.

The temptation to believe that this is a true-to-life portrait of Paul is almost irresistible. And although it is unlikely to have been painted before the fourth century, there is a respectable case to be made to support that idea. For eastern Christians religious pictures are much more than an art form; the tradition behind icons is based on the belief that an image can make a holy person a real presence in your church or your house, and a faithful representation of the original is the means by which that is achieved. Surely here in Ephesus, where Paul spent such a significant amount of his time during his missionary years and where he played such a full part in public life, there is a real chance that a visual record like this is rooted in memories of the man himself?

The artist has taken some significant liberties with tradition. The only written account of Paul's appearance is to be found in *The Acts of Paul*, an apocryphal work of the late second century. Because this description was written around a hundred years after Paul's death it is has often been argued that it was based on the words of an eyewitness, and Paul is said to be "a man of little stature, bald, crooked in the legs, of good state of body, with eyebrows joining,

10

and nose somewhat hooked, full of grace; for sometimes he appeared like a man, and sometimes like an angel." The cave artist certainly knew *The Acts of Paul;* they tell the story of the heroism of Thecla, one of his converts, and Thecla, in the form of a handsome Roman matron, looks out of the cave wall next to the apostle. But Paul's portrait here bears no relation at all to the famous description; in the Ephesus cave his eyebrows are quite separate, and he is far from bald. It would seem that the artist was confident that he knew best. Was he basing his representation on an earlier source, one closer, perhaps, to St. Paul himself?

The truth of course is that we shall probably never know. Paul's appearance, like so many other things about his life, is almost certainly lost to us forever. But the itch to look him in the eye across the centuries is always there. Anyone who sets out in search of St. Paul is driven by exactly the kind of feelings that inspire the veneration of an icon. If we can grasp the physical facts about him, if we can capture the life story that anchors him in our world of time and space, perhaps we shall be able to touch his genius and understand his mind.

And we know more about Paul as a historical figure than anyone else in the New Testament—or at least we think we do. Here is what his entry might have looked like in a first-century *Who's Who* of the Roman Empire:

> Born, AD 5, Tarsus, Asia Minor. Educated, University of Tarsus and School of Gamaliel, Jerusalem. Profession, Tentmaker. Nationality, Jewish with Roman Citizenship. Career, persecutor of Christians. Has vision of risen Christ 34. Makes missionary journey to Cyprus and Galatia 45–48, meets apostles in Jerusalem 49, establishes first Christian Churches in Asia Minor and the Balkans 49–56, imprisoned in Rome 59. Publications, 13 out of the 27 books of the New Testament.

The problem is that every single one of those dates and many of those facts are open to dispute. The moment you start looking more closely at the outline of Paul's life the edges become blurred. His date of birth, for example, is pure conjecture—some scholars put it much later, perhaps as late as AD 15.

We have a little more to go on when it comes to his place of birth. It is identified in the Acts of the Apostles, which is effectively his first biography; the author has his hero tell the mob in Jerusalem "I am a Jew, born in Tarsus in Cilicia" (Acts 22:3). There are several other references to Tarsus as his home and the city he returns to when he wants to lie low. But in his letters Paul himself never once mentions it. Why not? And does that mean the Acts of the Apostles cannot be trusted on this point? Before we have got through the first item in Paul's CV we confront a dilemma that has bedeviled all of modern Pauline scholarship: how much of the Acts of the Apostles can we believe, and how far does the picture of Paul it gives us square with the Paul we find in his own letters?

The question is so fundamental that it makes sense to deal with it before going any further. This debate stirs strong passions, not least because it touches on profound issues relating to the nature of biblical truth, and the sheer volume of the scholarly ink expended on the subject is daunting. After wading through page after page of dense and heavily footnoted text with a steadily sinking heart, I came to a cheering conclusion. The experts are so much at odds with one another that it seems perfectly reasonable to admit to being confused; scholarship alone is not enough to see us through.

It is generally accepted that the Acts of the Apostles was written by the same author as the Gospel according to St. Luke, and the two are often regarded as "the two volumes of a single work that today we should call 'a history of the rise of Christianity'"; thus Luke's Gospel is addressed to one Theophilus, and the prologue to Acts begins with the words, "In the first book, Theophilus, I wrote about all that Jesus did and taught from the beginning until the day when he was taken up to heaven, after giving instructions through the Holy Spirit to the apostles whom he had chosen" (Acts 1:1–2)—a fairly neat summation of the Gospel that has gone before. There is a long-established tradition that the Luke who wrote these two seminal texts was a doctor and one of Paul's friends; the letters ascribed to Paul in the New Testament do indeed include a reference to "Demas, and Luke, my fellow workers" (Phlm 24) and "Luke, the beloved physician" (Col 4:14), and the narrative of Acts sometimes switches into the first person "we," so that it reads as if the author and Paul are traveling together. The trouble is that Acts was almost certainly written in the 80s and 90s of the first century—sufficiently long after Paul's death to make it highly unlikely that their author was an eyewitness to the events they describe, let alone a friend of the apostle's.

Some scholars, particularly those of earlier generations, have chosen to regard the Acts of the Apostles as history in the modern sense, and have argued that you can read it as Paul's biography in the way that you would read a biography of a contemporary public figure. Here, for example, is the view of Sir William Ramsay, one of the titans of Pauline scholarship, writing in the late nineteenth century: "Our hypothesis is that Acts was written by a great historian, a writer who set himself to record the facts as they occurred, a strong partisan, indeed, but raised above partiality by his perfect confidence that he only had to record the facts as they occurred to make the truth of Christianity and the honour of Paul apparent."

Contrast that with the view of Donald Harman Akenson, Professor of History at Queen's University in Canada, writing a century later—Akenson calls Paul by the Jewish name Saul, which the apostle used before his conversion: "Except for those sections that are confirmed by Saul's (Paul's) letters, the rest of Acts (insofar as Saul is concerned), as a source of direct historical evidence has to be jettisoned." These two scholars stand at the extremes of the debate, but they illustrate the problem facing any unwary amateur who approaches this subject.

Harman Akenson's skepticism is based on the judgment that the Acts of the Apostles is "an extended ideological message"—that Luke was more the spin doctor than the physician of church tradition. He argues that we should always assume that the letters are the better source—because they are written by the man himself—and that when Acts can be judged against the letters it is often found wanting. This is his criticism of the traditional approach to Acts:

13

(1) When the Acts of the Apostles is contradicted by the letters of Saul, the letters are taken as accurate and the Acts of the Apostles as inaccurate; and (2) when they agree, Acts is taken as an historically useful amplification of the letters. Each of these procedures is solid, but procedure (3) most certainly does not follow; that when, as occurs on most matters of chronology and facticity, there is neither contradiction nor affirmation, the Acts are taken as being trustworthy. Consider what that method of evidence-cum-faith would mean for every day life: if you caught a co-worker lying to you a fair amount of the time—not all the time, for sometimes he or she says things that are indeed true—but in a significant portion of instances, on occasions when his or her word could not be checked, would you automatically accept as your presumption that the uncheckable instances are true? Not if you valued your position.

The only sensible way I can see to make my own mind up about this question is to rely on journalistic instinct. To any journalist, Professor Akenson's skepticism would seem entirely healthy. "Always go with the eyewitness" is a pretty good rule of thumb. But a journalist would also point out that people can sometimes lie about themselves, or at least put a spin on the facts, especially when they are trying to argue a case, as St. Paul so often is. So Paul's letters need to be treated with a degree of caution too.

Equally, few journalists would dismiss a document altogether simply because it is written with an ideological or propaganda purpose. Very often that is all we have to work with. I did several tours of duty in Iraq during the first Gulf crisis, and when Saddam Hussein gave one of his interminable speeches on Iraqi television, we would pull it apart to expose its internal contradictions and explore his political motivation, but we certainly would not ignore it, often for the very good reason that we had nothing else to report. Equally, a statement from the White House merits close attention despite the Bush administration's reputation for control and relying on the spin doctor's art; we may check it against independently verifiable facts from other sources, solicit opinion from other political figures on its veracity, and challenge its contents, but we are unlikely to throw it in the dustheap. For similar reasons it would be mad to ignore the Acts of the Apostles altogether; there is a truth in there somewhere, even if we have to search shrewdly to get at it. And for the record, I do not for a moment mean to suggest any kind of direct comparison between St. Luke and Saddam Hussein or Karl Rove. Apart from anything else, Luke was a much better storyteller—Acts is chock full of gripping tales, well worth reporting and reflecting on, however dubious their relationship to reality.

So trust the letters and read the Acts of the Apostles with some skepticism. But which letters? The view of Paul through the reversed telescope of history is further obscured by the fact that some of the letters included in the canon of the Bible under Paul's name were almost certainly written by other people. Here again the lessons of journalism are useful: expert opinion is there to be ransacked shamelessly, and common sense is often the most useful journalistic tool of all. There is no complete scholarly consensus, but the prevailing expert view, based on an analysis of the way language is used in the letters, is that the following are genuine: Romans, 1 Corinthians, 2 Corinthians, Galatians, Philippians, 1 Thessalonians, Philemon. And the following are bogus (bogus in the sense that Paul himself did not write them, which does not mean they are without value): Ephesians, Colossians, 2 Thessalonians, 1 Timothy, 2 Timothy, Titus.

By and large, common sense supports the experts' opinion. The First Letter to the Thessalonians, for example, is full of references to the imminent end of the world. It gives a vivid sense of the enthusiasm with which Paul looked forward to the moment when the risen Christ would appear without warning as "a thief in the night," and that the world as we know it would end. The second, however, reads like a huge excuse for the fact that the events predicted in the first have not taken place. The writer pleads with his audience not to get excited too soon: "we beg you, brothers and sisters, not to be quickly shaken in mind or alarmed, either by spirit or by word or by letter, as though from us, to the effect that the day of the Lord is already here" (2 Thess 2:1–2). The experts have concluded that this letter was written long after Paul's death as part of a campaign to deal with the awkward fact that the end of the world had not in fact arrived as billed. Common sense says that judgment squares entirely with the facts.

There will of course be those to whom this approach to St. Paul is blasphemous; those who believe that every one of the letters included in the biblical canon is written by Paul, that every one of the apostle's words is inspired by God and therefore true in the most literal sense, and that the Acts of the Apostles has the same absolute authority, being part of the Bible and therefore the Word of God.

To believe this involves exhausting intellectual yoga. Writers like Ramsay erect the most elaborate and ingenious structures to reconcile the story of Acts with St. Paul's own words, and while you cannot help admiring the depth of their research into the language and history of the first century and the sheer fleetness of intellectual foot on display, they are ultimately unconvincing. Furthermore one of the most attractive characteristics of Paul's own writing is the passion that drives his arguments; often it takes him into all sorts of apparently contradictory positions, sometimes within the same letter. To try and read the letters as literal, universal, and absolute truth is such a painful process that it strangles away all real meaning.

To accept that is not to dismiss the idea that God was at work in the apostle's life and writing. Father Scott Brodeur, who is the Professor of Pauline Theology at the Gregorian University in Rome, has spent much of his life wrestling with the apparent contradictions between his work as a biblical scholar and historian and his faith as a Roman Catholic priest. "God is the author of the Bible, absolutely true," he says, "but God called human authors and these human authors wrote in the light of their experience. God takes our human experience seriously and respects it and acts through it." In other words historical (and indeed journalistic) exploration of the Bible is perfectly compatible with religious belief and, to be blunt about it, it is not unreasonable for God to expect us to do a bit of work to get at his truth.

The classic journalistic questions are "Who? What? Where? When?"—if you read any well-written piece of wire copy from an agency like Reuters or the Press Association you will find

16

those questions are addressed within the first couple of paragraphs. But the really interesting journalistic questions are the ones that come next: "Why? What next? What does an event *mean*?" Those of course are the questions addressed in the analysis columns and the editorials, and most of the answers we read in our daily papers are, inevitably, speculative, because they are dealing with contemporary events with an uncertain outcome. But in St. Paul's case, they are in some ways easier to deal with than the "Who? What? Where? When?" questions because his influence has been felt in so many ways over so many centuries. Anyone who tries to write Paul's biography quickly comes to realize that they must be modest in their ambitions to answer the journalist's basic questions. The bigger question— "What does Paul mean?" in the broadest sense of the word—is the real focus for this book.

So let us look more closely at the idea that Paul was born in Tarsus, because my journalistic nose tells me it can offer some helpful clues in the search for answers to those deeper journalistic questions. The city, like Paul, belongs to that frustrating realm that hovers between legend and history. H. V. Morton describes arriving there in the 1930s in *In the Steps of St. Paul*, his wonderfully evocative and gloriously period classic:

> We took a carriage and drove for some way down a long, straight road and into a shabby little town where rows of wooden shacks faced each other across roadways of hard mud. And this was Tarsus, this dusty malarial little town crouched in a swamp.
>
> I looked for something that might have lingered from the time of its pride, but there was nothing. Invasion, war, and centuries of inertia have obliterated every vestige of the past. I was told that remains of the ancient city lie fifteen and twenty feet beneath the surface of modern Tarsus. People digging in their cellars and back-yards have felt their spades strike hard against the crowns of arches and the capitals of columns buried in the earth.

It is not quite as grim as that today, but there is little enough to bear witness to its history. In Acts, Paul famously describes Tarsus as "an important city" (Acts 21:39). Certainly it was of ancient origin; Islamic tradition holds that it was founded by Seth, the son of Adam, and classical mythology has its name derived from a hoof *(tarsos)* that the winged horse Pegasus lost there. Modern excavations have demonstrated it existed during the early Bronze Age (between 3000 and 2500 BC). In the fourth century BC, Xenophon, in a phrase echoed by Paul's epithet, called Tarsus "a great and prosperous city," and Alexander the Great saved it from Persian troops in 333 BC (he fell seriously ill there, apparently after taking a dip in the notoriously icy waters of the river Cydnus). But the event for which Tarsus is perhaps best remembered occurred around half a century before Paul's birth.

In 41 BC, Mark Antony was resting in the city—fresh from his victory at Philippi and a triumphal progress through Asia Minor—when he decided to send for Cleopatra, queen of Egypt. At twenty-eight, with a relationship with Caesar already under her belt, she probably had a shrewd idea what to expect from a victorious Mark Antony, who was not best pleased by her support for Cassius. Accordingly, she dressed to impress. And the manner of her arrival for the meeting—recorded by Plutarch and much improved by Shakespeare—must surely have been carefully calculated.

> The barge she sat in, like a burnish'd throne,
> Burned upon the water; the poop was beaten gold,
> Purple the sails, and so perfumed, that
> The winds were love-sick with them, the oars were silver,
> Which to the tune of flutes kept stroke, and made
> The water which they beat to follow faster,
> As amorous of their strokes. For her own person,
> It beggar'd all description; she did lie
> In her pavilion—cloth of gold of tissue—
> O'er picturing that Venus where we see
> The fancy outwork nature; on each side her
> Stood pretty dimpled boys, like smiling Cupids,
> With divers coloured fans, whose wind did seem

A Child of His Time

To glow the delicate cheeks which they did cool,
And what they undid did.

However fanciful Shakespeare's account may be, there seems
little doubt that one of the great romantic encounters of the
ancient world—with such profound political consequences—took
place in Tarsus a generation or so before Paul's birth. Let your
imagination play for a moment or two with the thought that this
scene was described to him by someone who actually saw it, and
you are reminded of one of the most obvious but nonetheless
essential facts about Paul's life and his mind: the backdrop of the
Hellenistic and Roman classical worlds is every bit as necessary to
understanding him as is the legacy of Judaism.

Paul may not mention Tarsus in his letters but there is plenty
in the way he wrote them to suggest St. Luke is right about his
birthplace. Strabo, who wrote his *Geography* of the ancient world
around the time of Paul's birth, records:

> The people of Tarsus have devoted themselves so
> eagerly, not only to philosophy, but also the whole
> round of education in general, that they have surpassed
> Athens, Alexandria or any other place that can be
> named where there have been schools and lecturers of
> philosophers....Further the city of Tarsus has all kinds
> of schools of rhetoric, and in general it not only has a
> flourishing population but also is the most powerful,
> thus keeping up the reputation of the mother-city.

If there is one thing that comes across in Paul's letters it is a
sense of intellectual enthusiasm; they are very much the words of
a man who grew up in a place where ideas matter, and Strabo's
Tarsus sounds like a first-century BC Oxford or Cambridge.
Although Paul wrote in *koine* Greek—the language of the street
rather than the language of Plato—his letters stand out as remarkable works of Greek literature, quite apart from their status as religious texts. Gilbert Murray, Regius Professor of Greek for thirty
golden years at Oxford, called him "one of the great figures of
Greek literature." We have no direct evidence whatsoever that

Paul was educated at one of the "schools of rhetoric" in his native city, but the way he writes suggests that the distinction "MA, Tarsus" would sit comfortably after his name. It is one of the qualities that make him a uniquely compelling figure to those who have seen Western civilization as a legacy that mixes Jewish religion, Greek thought, and Roman energy and order—like the nineteenth-century poet and essayist Matthew Arnold, who wrote extensively about St. Paul.

Strabo's description of Tarsus also suggests a certain self-confidence among its people. The city's coins bore the words "TARSUS, METROPOLIS, FIRST, FAIREST, AND BEST," rather in the way that license plates in the United States declare "New Hampshire, the Granite State," "Virginia is for Lovers," or even "Idaho, the Potato State." H. V. Morton claims, in characteristically muscular manner, that "it is important to realise that Paul was not born in the lassitude of an Oriental city, but the proud and virile atmosphere of mental and physical achievement." It is one of those asides that reveal much more about the writers about Paul than they do about Paul himself, but no one could write in the way Paul does—or indeed do the things he did—without a strong measure of self-belief.

Another picture of Tarsus—slightly less flattering but charming nonetheless—is painted by Flavius Philostratus in his *Life of Apollonius*. His hero—a contemporary of Paul's who became a Pythagorean philosopher with pretensions to magical powers—was taken to Tarsus to study philosophy, but was disgusted by what he found:

> the city harsh and strange and little conducive to the philosophic life, for nowhere are men more addicted than here to luxury: jesters and full of insolence are they all; and they attend more to their fine linen than the Athenians did to wisdom; and a stream called the Cydnus runs through their city, along the banks of which they sit like so many water-fowl.

There is something very appealing about the image of the Tarsians lounging on the banks of their clear cold river, well dressed and full of satirical wit, gossiping and chattering "like water-fowl." They sound as cynical and savvy as twenty-first-century New Yorkers. And Paul is a quintessentially urban figure. Father Scott Brodeur—himself a rather dapper citizen of the very stylish urban environment of Rome after many years in the city—says, "Paul fascinates me as an intellectual.... He is so extraordinarily international, so cosmopolitan. He loves cities. Here the contrast is between Paul and Jesus. Jesus is a man of the country—his first disciples are fishermen. Paul is an intellectual of the city."

For anyone who has had a conventional Christian upbringing, the overwhelming difference between Jesus and Paul is that one was divine and the other was not. But if you can move your mental furniture around radically enough to put that aside for a moment or two, the differences to which Father Brodeur refers are very striking indeed. Almost all the best-known stories of the gospels take place in rural or semirural settings. We meet Jesus walking by the Sea of Galilee, strolling through cornfields on the Sabbath, and withdrawing into the hills to appoint his apostles. It is only really during his final Passion that we get a sense of him in the metropolitan setting of Jerusalem—even during his ministry in the city his parables are about fig trees and vineyards. The way he talks and teaches is permeated by a sense of the countryside, and the very form of the parable has a simple rustic feel—especially if you set it against the kind of sophisticated, sometimes logic-chopping ratiocination of a Pauline letter. Paul, by contrast, is almost always presented to us in a cityscape—arguing in a marketplace, or preaching in a synagogue. He was an urban creature through and through, at a time when city culture expressed all that was best, brightest, and new about the civilization of the age.

And he was of course—if St. Luke is to be believed—a Roman citizen. The Acts of the Apostles reports that on a number of occasions Paul played the powerful citizenship card to get out of trouble. There is the memorable moment when he is strapped down waiting to be flogged and demands of the centurion on duty, "Is it legal to for you to flog a Roman citizen who is uncondemned?" The centurion summons his boss, the tribune, who seems rather put out by the news that his prisoner has such an elevated status. "'It cost me a large sum of money to get my citizenship," he remarks, ill-temperedly. "But I was born a citizen," comes the magisterial reply from Paul (Acts 22:25, 28).

All sorts of ingenious theories have been put forward to explain why a Jewish family from Tarsus should have been granted the privilege of Roman citizenship. Father Jerome Murphy O'Connor, one of the most respected of Paul's modern biographers, suggests Cleopatra's Antony may have used citizenship as a bribe to secure Jewish support in Tarsus during the civil wars. In his life of Paul, A. N. Wilson finds a clue in the fact that Paul is said to have been a tentmaker, and speculates that the family could have been rewarded for providing winter quarters for Mark Antony's troops. And of course it is possible that Paul's father was a freed slave who acquired Roman citizenship from his master.

The trouble, once again, is that Paul himself never at any point mentions his citizenship—which is odd, because there are several passages in the letters when he breaks off to tell his readers a bit about himself and his background. There does not seem any particular reason to be skeptical about Luke on this score, but Paul's citizenship is another of those "facts" about his life that we think we know but cannot really be entirely sure about. What we can say for certain—and here the letters do support the Acts of the Apostles—is that he was very much a man of the Roman Empire, who moved around its roads and cities with a strong sense of being at home. *Koine* Greek was a cross-cultural passport in the way that English is today, Acts has Paul astonishing the Jews of Jerusalem with his command of Aramaic, and the way his frequent encounters with Roman officials are described suggests he probably spoke Latin as well. Roman citizen or not in the formal sense, St. Paul certainly seems to have been a full citizen of the known world in spirit—and in the first century the known world meant the Roman Empire.

There have been those who even questioned whether Paul was a Jew; this seems to take skepticism to the point of silliness. In contrast to his silence on the subject of his birthplace and his citizenship, Paul is vocal about his parentage, making it explicitly clear that he was born into a religiously observant Jewish family. It is a theme that surfaces again and again in his letters, and his tortured relationship with Judaism is one of the principle narratives driving his life and thought.

There remains, of course, the intriguing question of how Paul and his family wound up in Tarsus. Writing in the fourth century, St. Jerome offers this explanation—it does not seem to be offered with great conviction, but it has acquired the status of church tradition:

> We have heard this story. They say that the parents of the Apostle Paul were from Gischala, a region of Judea, and that when the whole province was devastated by the hand of Rome and the Jews scattered throughout the world, they moved to Tarsus, a town in Cilicia; the adolescent Paul inherited the personal status of his parents.

There is of course no direct historical evidence whatever to support this tradition, but like so many of the uncertain stories that surround Paul's early life it serves as a reminder of an essential fact that is certain: Paul was a Diaspora Jew. And if the tradition is right he would have inherited a folk memory of a violent upheaval that drove his family into exile. It puts him in the great tradition of exiled Jews who have made such extraordinary contributions to the history of thought and religion—from Moses before him to Marx so many centuries later.

The evidence we have about Paul's immediate family is very dodgy indeed. A mysterious nephew pops up in the final chapters of Acts. Paul has escaped the mob and is under Roman arrest when a group of Jews decide to kill him. "Now the son of Paul's sister heard about the ambush; so he went and gained entrance to the barracks and told Paul" (Acts 23:16). We hear nothing more anywhere about this character—or indeed about his mother or any other siblings Paul may or may not have had. There is no particular reason to doubt the Acts here, but the mysterious nephew does seem a suspiciously convenient narrative device, and the information about him is so scanty that it is not particularly useful.

In Paul's own letters there is a tantalizing reference to a mother; he sends greetings to "Rufus, chosen in the Lord, and his mother and mine" (Rom 16:13). But some translations (including the NRSV, which I have used throughout this book) render this rather differently: "Rufus, chosen in the Lord, and greet his mother—a mother to me also," and that seems to make more sense; if Paul really was sending greetings to his own mother she would surely have been at the top of the list rather then buried halfway down as an afterthought to Rufus. And again, even if Paul is referring to his natural mother, this one reference does not take us very far.

The question of Paul's social class was a source of particular fascination to Victorian and early twentieth-century writers. There is no getting round the fact that by Luke's account Paul was a manual laborer—in Corinth the apostle meets a couple called Aquila and Priscilla, "and because he was of the same trade, he stayed with them, and they worked together—by trade they were tentmakers." But those who find it difficult to believe that such a pivotal figure in the history of humankind should have been "in trade" and worked with his hands incline to the view that he was a tentmaker in the sense that the Rothschilds are winemakers. Sir William Ramsay is particularly enjoyable to read on this subject. Paul's Roman citizenship, he suggests, "may be taken as proof that his family was one of distinction and at least moderate wealth." He sternly refutes any suggestion that Paul's family were recent immigrants to the city—they were, it seems, an old Tarsian family, who could trace their origins back to the Seleucid kings. The apostle's statement in his Letter to the Philippians that he had given up all for Christ ("For his sake I have suffered the loss of all things, and I regard them as rubbish" Phil 3:8) is taken as a reference to some terrible family row that cost Paul his patrimony: "These emphatic words suit the mouth of one who had been disowned by his family, and reduced from a position of wealth and influence in his nation to poverty and contempt," Sir William concludes.

Ramsay's German near-contemporary Adolf Deissmann takes quite the opposite view:

The tentmaker Paul ought certainly not be thought of as a learned writer of books who to refresh himself from his brainwork would sit for an hour or two working as an amateur at the loom. Nor ought he to be disfigured with the bombastic-comical title "tent-manufacturer," as though the artisan missionary was a disgrace to a Christianity become respectable. Rather he was a simple man who as a journeyman worked at his trade for wages, which were the basis for his economic existence.

The temptation to project one's own prejudices and worldview on Paul is overwhelming. It would help us so much to get a sense of who he really was if we could imagine him speaking posh or estuary English, give him an old-school tie or a sad story of growing up in Tarsus's back-to-back terraces. Honesty compels us to recognize that we can never really go beyond the paradox of a man who worked with his hands but used language with all the skills of a lawyer, the power of a politician, and the grace of a poet.

Paul is in fact a bundle of paradoxes: a Jewish zealot who enjoyed citizenship of the empire that oppressed the Jews, a passionate monotheist who could argue like a Greek philosopher, and of course both Christianity's first recorded persecutor and one of its founding fathers. What really matters about his background in Tarsus is that it illuminates his role as a kind of cultural and religious vortex—a point at which all sorts of different currents from the past came together. Paul, "all things to all men," as he put it, spun the different threads of his history into something new and richly fertile, and hurled it into the future.

It would be wrong to leave Paul's early life behind without a word or two about sex—a source of constant and even obsessive fascination to almost all those who have sought to interpret his life and writing.

Jerome Murphy O'Connor has created a wife for Paul. He argues that the young Paul, trying to make his way in the world, would have done everything he could to fit in with Jewish norms—and that that would have meant marrying before reaching twenty. Paul states explicitly that he is single by the time of his missions, so Murphy O'Connor suggests that his family could have been killed in an earthquake or by an outbreak of plague, and he advances the argument that the trauma would provide a psychological explanation for the violence of Paul's early anti-Christian persecution.

Murphy O'Connor concedes the highly speculative nature of this series of propositions, and this is one of those occasions when the letters may help us towards the truth. In the famous passage on marriage in his First Letter to the Corinthians, Paul writes: "To the unmarried and the widows I say that it is well for them to remain unmarried as I am. But if they are not practicing self-control, they should marry. For it is better to marry than to be aflame with passion" (1 Cor 7:8–9).

The tone as much as the content is what is so striking about that passage. There is a coolness and indifference there that it is difficult to square with the experience of actually being married—particularly if the marriage ended in the traumatic way that Murphy O'Connor suggests. Even Paul's more positive comments about the way a relationship should work within marriage have a strangely impersonal feel about them.

That is in sharp contrast to the way Paul refers to friendships. When he uses his letters to send his greetings to particular individuals—as he does, for example, towards the end of the Letter to the Romans—there is a sense of real personal affection in the way he does it. The Letter to Philemon is by far the shortest of those that have come down to us, but it is a vivid fragment of real life and a document of great tenderness. Paul, in prison (probably in Ephesus) has apparently been looked after by a runaway slave, Onesimus, and is sending him back to his master, who is clearly one of Paul's friends and fellow Christians. He pleads to Philemon that Onesimus should not only be forgiven but elevated from the status of slave to that of "brother": "though I am bold enough in Christ to command you to do your duty, yet I would rather appeal to you on the basis of love—and I, Paul, do this as an old man and now also as a prisoner of Christ Jesus. I am appealing to you for my child, Onesimus, whose father I have become during my imprisonment" (Phlm 8–10). The strength and delicacy of his feelings toward both slave and master are palpable.

A Child of His Time

To me Paul's letters read like the work of a bachelor with a talent for friendship—a thoroughly gregarious fellow, in fact, despite the occasional outbreaks of towering rage. Many people have speculated that he must have had a miserable childhood, but the warmth that sometimes breaks through in his letters must derive from somewhere. Whenever I think of the world in which he grew up my imagination inevitably bathes it in sunlight, and Adolf Deissmann paints a wonderfully evocative picture of the Aegean, which "enabled men to grow up in light and air, men of wide open soul who were able to interpret the voices of heaven and the riddles of Hades."

There is, however, no doubt that there is also a strong sense of a darker side to Paul's nature in the letters. It comes through especially clearly in an agonized passage in the Letter to the Romans: "I was once alive apart from the law; but when the commandment came, sin revived and I died, and the very commandment that promised life proved to be the death to me. For sin, seizing an opportunity in the commandment, deceived me and through it killed me" (Rom 7:9–11).

It seems that Paul's experience of learning the Torah as an adolescent was irrevocably bound up with a sense of guilt; as he became aware of the demands God's law made on him he became equally aware of his own inability to live up to them:

> For I do not do what I want, but I do the very thing I hate.... So I find it to be a law that when I want to do what is good, evil lies close at hand. For I delight in the law of God in my inmost self, but I see in my members another law at war with the law of my mind, making me captive of the law of sin that dwells in my members. Wretched man that I am! (Rom 7:15, 21–24)

Hugh Schonfield in *The Jew of Tarsus: An Unorthodox Portrait of Paul* suggests that Paul "had become early obsessed with a secret guilt complex, which he was unable to shake off..." and recognizes the emotion from his own "fairly orthodox" Jewish childhood:

What twinges of conscience there were over sharpening a pencil on the Sabbath! What a problem of faith was raised by attending synagogue in one's school cap because the badge was a Maltese cross! If, surrounded with care and affection, these matters could trouble the soul of a London lad in the twentieth century, how much more, without these advantages, would similar issues affect a Jewish boy of pagan Tarsus in the first century.

When we first meet Paul as an agent actively engaged with the world rather than a bundle of speculative legends, he is not in Tarsus but in Jerusalem, and there is something eating his soul.

2

Paul the Jew

In January 1986, with the snow lying deep on the streets of New York outside, I was woken at 4 a.m. in my hotel room by a call from London: could I please fly to Miami, buy a set of tropical clothes, and charter a private jet to Haiti? There was a coup, and the program wanted it covered.

The revolution that ended the long reign of the Duvalier family quickly turned nasty. The night before I managed to reach the island, Jean-Claude Duvalier—known as "Baby Doc" in deference to "Papa Doc," the father from whom he inherited power over this history-haunted grave of hope—fled into exile. Almost before the fugitive dictator's plane had tucked its wheels away after take-off there were crowds of crudely armed men on the streets of Port-au-Prince, looking for vengeance for three decades of repression.

The obvious targets were the Tontons Macoutes, the secret police set up by Papa Doc in the 1950s. Their nickname derived from the voodoo bogeyman of Haitian folklore who steals children in his knapsack, and with their trademark dark glasses and machetes they turned a scary story that mothers told their children into a real-life nightmare for adults. Graham Greene gave them a sinister fictional immortality in his novel *The Comedians*.

A couple of mornings after I arrived in Haiti, one of the camera crews I was working with turned a corner in Port-au-Prince and stumbled on a Tonton being stoned. As we crowded round the edit machine to watch the footage being played back, one American producer breathed in awed tones, "My God, the bad guys are really getting it this time." It seemed a curiously simplistic response to the scene we were watching. What struck me was the sheer energy and endurance needed to kill the man; he kept trying to get up, again and again, despite the stones raining down on him, and even after the mob had hit him often enough to stop him staggering to his feet they had to set about their work with some vigor before his torso finally flopped backwards onto the ground for the last time. To kill someone by stoning you really have to hate them—with a passion.

Passion and hatred drive the mob that kills St. Stephen, the first Christian martyr, in the grisly stoning recounted by St. Luke in the Acts of the Apostles. For Jews in St. Paul's time, three crimes merited this extreme sanction—blasphemy, adultery, and the violation of the Sabbath. Stoning as a religiously sanctioned punishment in the Jerusalem of the first century should have been more carefully ritualized than it was in Haiti in the 1980s. The victim was supposed to be thrown off a cliff or a high wall first— the coup de grâce could be more easily delivered to someone who was unconscious. But Luke's account of the stoning of St. Stephen suggests he came in for something closer to the treatment meted out to the Tonton Macoute. He was dragged out of the city by the mob and was conscious enough to say his prayers while the crowd chucked rocks at him. "While they were stoning Stephen," says Acts, "he prayed, 'Lord Jesus, receive my spirit.' Then he knelt down and cried out in a loud voice, 'Lord, do not hold this sin against them.' When he had said this, he died" (Acts 7:59–60).

The first time we meet Paul in Acts he is watching this scene, and he was evidently rather more than a casual bystander; "the witnesses laid their coats at the feet of a young man named Saul," writes Luke, using the future apostle's preconversion name, and "Saul approved of their killing him" (Acts 7:58; 8:1). He then joins with enthusiasm—or perhaps even leads—a wholesale crack-down on Stephen's fellow Christians: "Saul was ravaging the church by entering house after house; dragging off both men and women, he committed them to prison" (Acts 8:3).

Some of Paul's apologists suggest that this is one of those occasions when Luke plays fast and loose with the facts to make a point; for Paul's subsequent conversion to Christ to have its full impact, runs the argument, the reader needs to be given a dramatic sense of his earlier commitment to the anti-Christian cause. The idea that Paul's presence at the stoning of Stephen is a kind of literary device is lent some force by the fact that this is the first time Luke introduces him; it is a very dramatic entry, and profoundly shocking, as it is presumably meant to be. And anyway, says the voice of common sense, this is the man who later declared that "Love is patient; love is kind; love is not envious or boastful or arrogant or rude. It does not insist on its own way" (1 Cor 13:4–5). His writing so often lights up with tenderness and humanity to those around him that it seems almost inconceivable that he could really have behaved in this barbaric way. But I have a nasty suspicion that he could indeed have.

Paul is too big a figure for us to make excuses for him; he is a seductive character for those who engage with his ideas, but that makes it all the more important for us to be clear-eyed about his failings and the more malign side of his impact on history. He never himself mentions the martyrdom of Stephen in his letters, so the incident has to remain in that uncertain realm where the old BBC rule of "two sources" can never be met. But the way he writes reveals a man who is acutely aware of the contradictions in his own character, and very self-conscious about the image he is presenting to his readers; any of us would be tempted to edit an incident like this out of our past.

Paul is, however, himself anxious to stress the strength of his early anti-Christian sentiments, telling the Galatians, "I was violently persecuting the church of God and was trying to destroy it" (Gal 1:13). As we shall see when we look more closely at some of the disputes he became caught up in during his missionary period, his passion for his faith quite easily tipped over into aggressive feelings about his opponents. Whether or not Paul actually witnessed the stoning of Stephen, his participation in such an event is entirely consistent with at least one face of the Paul that emerges from the letters. This ugly incident at the heart of the early Christian story needs to be unravelled—especially since that story has been stained so dreadfully by the blood of the persecuted in the centuries since then.

St. Stephen's Gate—where a somewhat uncertain tradition holds that the stoning took place—was rebuilt by the Ottomans in the sixteenth century; today it squats on the edge of Jerusalem's Old City, a brutal architectural assertion of imperial power. To understand what brought St. Paul here that day we have to understand a little of the long romance—often unconsummated—between the Jewish people and the land of Israel, and the special place that Jerusalem holds within that story.

This love affair is of course as old as the Jews themselves and, like all the best love stories, it kicks off in earnest with an extravagant gesture of devotion. When Abraham's wife Sarah dies, he is living in "the land of Canaan" in what is today the West Bank town of Hebron. He approaches the local people, the Hittites, "a stranger and an alien residing among you," and asks to buy a field to bury her. They offer it to him for free, but he insists on paying the full price: "I will give the price of the field; accept it from me" (Gen 23:13). It is a text much quoted by Israeli settlers in Hebron today. The cave of Machpelah on the field for which Abraham paid 40 shekels of silver became his own burial place too, and in the fullness of time he and Sarah were joined there by Isaac, Jacob, Rebecca, and Leah; this, the settlers will tell you, is the family vault of the Jewish people.

But it was King David who made the idea of a Promised Land a reality in a way that we can touch in history, and although he was so famously a great romantic his part in this love story has more to do with war and politics than anything else. He was first and foremost a great war leader, and he established the first Jewish state at the point of a sword. Like Otto von Bismarck and George Washington many centuries later, he had the political skills needed to build a nation on the back of a conflict. When America's founding fathers designed their new nation they faced the competing claims of the states, and found their solution in a neutral capital beyond the states' boundaries—Washington, D.C. In the same way David chose the city of Jebus as a focus to unite Israel's tribes. The Jebusites had frustrated the Israelites' attempts to take their city for two hundred years, so when David successfully laid siege there he could claim it as something new and freshly minted outside the history of Israel's tribes—his personal possession, "David's City."

David brought the Ark of the Covenant—the rough-and-ready wooden box containing the tablets handed down to Moses on

Mount Sinai—to Jerusalem, a first step toward making it a religious as well as a political center. He bought land for a temple, but—in one of those powerful metaphorical twists that weave religion and politics together in the Jewish story—the Bible tells us that he could not build it because he had "shed so much blood" (1 Chr 22:8). It was his son Solomon who cemented Jerusalem's place in his people's understanding of themselves through the construction of the First Temple, a building quite unlike anything in the Israelites' history.

It must have seemed almost pagan, with its 40-foot bronze pillars, gold-covered altar, elaborate baroque engravings, and cedar roof. In the Holy of Holies, protected by two cherubim, each with a wingspan of 18 feet, Solomon placed the Ark and (according to tradition) the staff of Moses, Aaron's rod, the manna jar, and the pillow on which Jacob's head rested when he had his dream. The Book of Kings records that once the Ark had been placed in the Temple "a cloud filled the house of the LORD," and that the "glory of the LORD filled the house of the LORD" (1 Kgs 8:10–11).

Any doubts about Solomon's objective to secure his royal authority on a new foundation of divine approval are dispelled by his address to the crowds at the opening ceremony for the Temple. Explicitly and very publicly he claims his Temple's right to be considered God's house; in his prayers he declares, "I have built you an exalted house, a place for you to dwell in forever" (1 Kgs 8:13). But Solomon is the most calculating of all the Bible's great characters; wary of the charge of blasphemy, he is careful to allow some ambiguity to creep into the idea that God actually lives in his Temple: "But will God indeed dwell on the earth?" he asks. "Even heaven and the highest heaven cannot contain you, much less this house that I have built" (1 Kgs 8:27). The message behind this episode remains clear: the religious as well as the political life of the Israelites is now centered on the king and his capital, Jerusalem.

It soon became unacceptable to sacrifice anywhere other than the Temple, and the altars in the "high places" where people had gathered in the half-pagan past fell into disuse. The process culminated in the reforms of Josiah, king of Judah, who ordered that all sacrifice outside Jerusalem should be outlawed and any remaining provincial temples should be closed down. Not long thereafter, the Temple was itself destroyed by the Babylonians, but a kind of marriage had now been solemnized between Jerusalem and the Jewish people. It has been a rocky relationship at times, but it has endured for millennia. Like any long marriage it has been formed over the years by its own joy and suffering, so that no one outside the relationship can fully understand it.

I got a glimpse of the meaning of Jerusalem to the Jews— and a glimpse is probably the best a non-Jew can hope for—by talking to Natan Sharansky, the Soviet dissident turned Israeli politician. To many of my generation, Sharansky and his kind were as close as you could come to modern heroes. Among all the uncertainties of the 1970s and '80s there was one thing no one really needed to argue about: the Soviet system was evil. The courage of the dissidents who stood up to it shone out as an example, uncomplicated by the shades of gray that make it so difficult to work out who are today's political heroes.

Sharansky's journey to become one of the most powerful symbols of dissent against the Soviet system was inextricably bound with the development of his sense of identity as a Jew. Born in the 1940s and brought up as an "assimilated" Jew, the young Sharansky got on with life inside the system like most of his generation of Soviet Jews, and graduated in mathematics from the Physical Technical Institute in Moscow. He describes the experience as leading a double life: "You vote, you read, you write in accordance with what you're told to," he remembers, "and at the same time you know that there is a different reality, about which you can speak only with your closest friends and your family." The turning point came with the Israeli triumphs of the Six Day War in 1967: "The anti-Semitic propaganda in the Soviet Union became even stronger," he told me, "but at the same time suddenly you found that even anti-Semites began to respect you...all these people around you connected you and your life with a country about which you knew practically nothing." It propelled him into a study of Judaism and Jewish history in which he kept encountering "the central role of Jerusalem" as something that "connects Jews all over the world," and, even more powerfully, "connects mankind with the idea of an ethical God." The image of Jerusalem—which he had, of course, never seen—and all it

Paul the Jew

symbolized sustained him when he was arrested and imprisoned in the gulags; he recalls reading the psalms in his cell and feeling that "King David himself...came to prison to tell me 'fear no evil.'" When he was finally released in an East-West prisoner exchange on the border of the then-divided Germany, he was given an Israeli passport and flown to the real Jerusalem—he describes it as a journey "from hell to paradise."

Sharansky's experience brings the contours of the Jewish romance with Jerusalem into especially dramatic relief, but the emotions that inspired him echo through all the stories of exile and diaspora that are such a leitmotiv of Jewish history. However comfortable Paul and his family were in the imperial Roman city of Tarsus, the young man who was so "zealous for the traditions of our ancestors" must have felt the same kind of pull toward David's City. We tend to think of the "Jewish Diaspora" as something that began when the Romans crushed the great Jewish revolt in the first century AD, but in Paul's time there were somewhere between seven and eight million Jews, and only around two and a half million lived in Palestine itself. The rest were scattered across the Roman Empire and beyond, and, like much of the modern Diaspora, they looked to Jerusalem as a focus for their religion and their sense of national identity. Paul was a Diaspora Jew in much the same way as an observant Jew born in New York or Manchester is today.

So the journey to Jerusalem was a natural one for Paul to make. But neither the Acts nor Paul's letters tell us exactly when or how the young Tarsian travelled to the holy city. We do not know whether he originally went on pilgrimage and stayed on, or set out with some kind of plan for pursuing his education and career. And, to muddy the waters further, there is one worrying sentence in his letters that could be read to contradict the whole of St. Luke's account of his time in Jerusalem as a young Jewish zealot. Paul tells the Galatians that at a period some time *after* his conversion he was "still unknown by sight to the churches of Judea" (Gal 1:22), which is difficult to square with the idea that he was one of their most prominent persecutors. Furthermore, most chronologies of Paul's life suggest that if he did study in Jerusalem he would have been there at the time of Jesus' mission

35

and crucifixion, and yet he never mentions any personal knowledge of or connection with Jesus' life.

Whatever Paul meant by that sentence in Galatians this seems to me one of those occasions where one has to give Luke the benefit of the doubt. If the whole Jerusalem episode in Paul's early life is an invention, it is a very elaborate one, and, to use a literary argument rather than a historical one, we need some kind of Jerusalem experience to make sense of the Paul we meet in his letters. Whatever doubts we may have about the accounts of the stoning of Stephen and Paul's work as a Temple policeman, they get us close to important truths about him, tying him to his Jewish heritage. And that is essential to an understanding of the theological revolution that the letters unfold.

The Jerusalem he would have found when he arrived there from Tarsus was dominated by one of the great wonders of the Roman world: the Temple of Herod. Like David's decision to establish his kingdom at Jerusalem, Herod's announcement to the pilgrims gathered for Passover in 20 BC was probably driven more by political calculation than anything else. One can imagine the stir in the crowd at the news that the Temple of Zerubbabel was to be restored and improved. This Second Temple (Solomon's was destroyed in 587 BC, after an abortive revolt against the Babylonians) had stood for half a millennium. Herod the Great had some ground to make up with his Jewish subjects; he took power in Jerusalem at the head of an army of 30,000 Roman infantry and 6,000 cavalry, and the fact that he had two of his sons judicially strangled provides a flavor of his leadership style. What more effective means could there be of establishing himself in the affections of the Jewish people (and indeed in their history) than the construction of a Temple that would outclass anything that the other religions of the day had to offer?

When I tried to enter the Temple Mount in the autumn of 2001 to get a sense of the scene St. Paul would have known, I was turned back by a nervous soldier at the end of a grubby little street in the Arab quarter of the Old City. "Muslims only," he muttered, flak-jacketed and flustered by the stupidity of a journalist who had forgotten that the whole area had been closed off since Ariel Sharon's visit there sparked a new Palestinian intifada a year earlier. If you stand for a while by the Western Wall in Jerusalem today—the Wailing Wall, which is all that survives of Herod's Temple—the massive size of the blocks of stone provides something for the imagination to work on. But it is almost impossible to recreate in our modern minds the impact of seeing Jerusalem and its Temple for the first time in the first century.

If the young Saul approached from the south he would have encountered Herod's most extravagant architectural flourish first. Flavius Josephus, the first-century Jewish historian, is almost breathless in his description of the cloister, "which deserves to be mentioned better than anything under the sun"; running along the south side of the Temple's outer courtyard, it rose so high above the valley that anyone looking down from the top "would be giddy, while his sight would not reach such an immense depth." The cloister was built a little like a Gothic cathedral, with two aisles and a central nave, although the side towards the Temple was open. The aisles were 30 feet wide and 50 high, the nave 100 feet high and close to 100 feet in breadth, and the whole was substantially longer than St. Peter's in Rome. It was supported by 162 columns in 4 rows, each so thick that "three men might, with their arms extended, fathom it round," and their "chapiters were made with sculptures after the Corinthian order, and caused an amazement by reason of the grandeur of the whole."

The Temple itself stood at the heart of a complex that extended over 35 acres, and was "visible to those that dwelt in the country for a great many furlongs." The front of the building "wanted nothing that was likely to surprise either men's minds or their eyes; for it was covered all over with plates of gold of great weight, and at the first rising of the sun reflected back a very fiery splendor." From a distance it looked like "a mountain covered with snow, for as to the parts of it that were not gilt, they were exceeding white." Its huge doors "were adorned with embroidered veils, with their flowers of purple, and pillars interwoven; and over all these, but under the crown work, was spread out a golden vine with its branches hanging down from a great height, the largeness and fine workmanship of which was an astonishing sight." Thousands of Jews from the Diaspora came on pilgrimage here every year, and whether they were from Hellenistic Asia

Minor, like Paul, from Alexandria or from Rome itself, Herod's Temple left them in no doubt that, in terms of religion at least, Jerusalem and the Jews were a world-class act.

Someone of Paul's vivid religious imagination must have been profoundly impressed by the way the Temple and its life were centered around the Law. The reminders of the overwhelming importance of purity were everywhere. The roof of the Temple building itself was covered in sharp spikes "to stop the pollution of it by birds sitting upon it." At the entrance to the inner courts there was a sign warning non-Jews to stay away on pain of death: "Let no Gentile enter within the balustrade and enclosure about the holy place and whosoever is caught let him be responsible for himself because death follows." Women were not allowed into the Temple during menstruation, and "those that had the gonorrhoea and the leprosy were excluded from the city entirely." And the poet and master of metaphor who emerges from Paul's letters must surely have been stirred by the rivers of red that flowed over the Temple's gleaming white marble and stone. Josephus records that at one Passover during Nero's time there were more than a quarter of a million animal sacrifices "from the ninth hour to the eleventh." Even if we allow for exaggeration and reduce that number by a factor of ten, it is still an astonishing figure. The Alexandrian Jew Aristeas describes 700 priests working away at the ritual butchery. At the base of the vast altar Aristeas observed "many openings for water...invisible to all except those making the sacrifices, so that all the blood is collected in great quantities and washed away in the twinkling of an eye."

Josephus tells us that there were three principle sects within Judaism during this period—the Essenes, the Pharisees, and the Sadducees. The Jerusalem of the first century was every bit as addicted to argument, religious and political, as is the Jerusalem of today, and a maelstrom of debate and factionalism seems to have swirled around the stately magnificence of the Temple. Paul explicitly tells us that before his conversion he was a Pharisee. The declaration comes in a curious passage in the Letter to the Philippians, one of those "Stephen-stoning" moments when his darker side is revealed as he suddenly whips out his sarcasm like a weapon (indeed the change of tone from the benign mood of

most of the letter is so abrupt that some scholars believe two letters have been bolted together here). "Beware of the dogs,
beware of the evil workers," he tells these first European
Christians, and, in an astonishingly snide reference to the Jewish
practice of circumcision, he goes on, "beware those who mutilate
the flesh" (Phil 3:2). But he then establishes his own Jewish cre-
dentials: "circumcised on the eighth day, a member of the people
of Israel, of the tribe of Benjamin, a Hebrew born of Hebrews; as
to the law, a Pharisee; as to zeal, a persecutor of the church; as to
righteousness under the law, blameless" (Phil 3:5).

The Pharisees get an extraordinarily bad press in the
Christian New Testament: "the Scribes and Pharisees" stand out
in the memory of hundreds of Sunday readings in church like
pantomime villains, automatically provoking a mental "boo"
and invariably confounded by the superior wisdom, wit, and
spirituality of Jesus. *Pharisee* in the gospels is almost a shorthand
for someone who is obsessively concerned with the petty forms
and the outward show of religious practice, and the word
Pharisaic was once routinely used to mean "hypocritical." Paul
himself contributes to the impression of Pharisaic self-righteous-
ness, fundamentalism, and self-importance by the way he writes
about his own past.

In fact the Pharisees seem to have been (and our knowledge
of their beliefs remains somewhat uncertain) the most moderate
of the movements identified by Josephus—who tried out all three
as a teenager before himself settling on the Pharisees as the group
which offered the most congenial kind of religion. The Essenes
were the ascetics, living in monastic communities along the desert
fringes, inspired by apocalyptic dreams; in some cases, like that of
the Qumran community of Dead Sea Scrolls fame, they actively
prepared for insurrection and guerrilla war. They considered
pleasure to be evil, remained celibate, and were probably misogy-
nists: "They guard against the lascivious behavior of women,"
writes Josephus, "and are persuaded that none of them preserve
their fidelity to one man." This continence may have been just as
well. Josephus records that the Essenes did not replace their
clothes until they were falling off their backs, and thought "to be
sweaty is a good thing."

The distinction between the Sadducees and the Pharisees seems to have revolved around their attitude to the Law, that absolutely central fact of Jewish life that was also to play such a central role in Paul's theological revolution. The word *law* is perhaps the nearest translation we have for *Torah* but it doesn't do justice to what it means for observant Jews. The literal meaning of Torah is "teaching," but that doesn't quite capture its full significance either, and like the power of Jerusalem as an idea and not just a place, it is probably something you can only fully appreciate if you have been brought up in a Jewish household. The leading Talmudic scholar Rabbi Adin Steinsaltz put it to me like this: "The Jewish religion embraces you from the moment you open your eyes, to the moment you go to sleep. There is no minute when you are free from it—from the time you are born, to the time you are buried, it never leaves you." The Torah covers, he explained, "how to sit, how to stand, how you're to wash your hands," and even how you go to the lavatory and what you do in bed with your spouse. Rabbi Steinsaltz is a chaotically bearded and terminally scruffy figure who seemed to be forever sucking at a recalcitrant pipe, and his transparent cheerfulness and good nature took some of the sting out of his swipe at Christianity:

> If you are a nice Christian, you treat God like an old father. You put him in a lavish home, and you tell him "Father, I love you. You stay here—you'll enjoy it, you'll enjoy the scenery, the birds, and so on. I promise I will come every week with the children to visit you. But you know...please don't visit me at home!" By contrast, Judaism interferes in our kitchen, in our pockets, in our bedrooms.

The foundation for the Torah is the lengthy set of instructions that God gave to Moses on Mount Sinai. The Sadducees were fundamentalist in their approach to this; they held that only what was written down was valid, and that nothing could be changed. This meant, for example, that Sadducees refused to accept the ideas of afterlife or resurrection, because they are not mentioned in the written law recorded by Moses. The Sadducees also appear to have been aristocrats—their name suggests they were descendants of Zadok, the great priest of David's era—and held a hereditary position in the workings of the Temple; perhaps not surprisingly they were rigid in their insistence on the centrality of the Temple in Jewish religious life.

The Pharisee movement emerged in the middle of the second century BC and was associated with a rise in popular Jewish education. Pharisees were every bit as scrupulous in their attachment to the Law as the Sadducees, but they believed in the idea of oral Law as well as written Law. God, they believed, had given Moses an oral Law on Mount Sinai that was not recorded in the Bible, but had been passed down from one generation to the next. This had one overwhelming intellectual advantage; it meant that the Law could be creatively reinterpreted to suit the times, and adapted to take account of change. Thus Pharisees did believe in resurrection, indeed their teaching on heaven and hell sounds remarkably similar to that which passed into Christian theology; those who had lived badly would be "contained in an everlasting prison," those who had lived well would "live again."

The Pharisaic concept of Law also made their teachers and thinkers—their rabbis—extremely powerful and important figures, because they had the job of interpreting the Torah. Two Pharisee rabbis stand out as especially influential figures. Hillel the Babylonian was active a generation before Paul would have been a student in Jerusalem, but the aphorism for which he is best known foreshadows both the teaching of Jesus and the approach to the Law that Paul came to adopt. When asked to sum up the whole Torah as briefly as possible, he said, "What is hateful to yourself, do not to another; that is the whole law, all the rest is commentary." It is a position very close to Jesus' answer to a Sadducee interrogator in St. Matthew's Gospel: "'You shall love the Lord your God with all your heart, and with all your soul, and with all your mind.' This is the greatest and first commandment. And a second is like it: 'You shall love your neighbor as yourself.' On these two commandments hang all the law and the prophets" (Matt 22:37–40).

Rabban Gamaliel is closely associated with Hillel by tradition, and it is sometimes said that he was his son or grandson. He is credited with liberalizing the strictures on remarriage after divorce. However he is also said to have given much thought to the question of what size a loaf should be ("Never in my father's house did they bake large loaves, only small ones") and whether Jews could use wineskins that had previously been used by Gentiles (he decided that it all depended on the shape of the tear: "When the tear in the hide is round, it is prohibited, when it is straight, it is permitted"). Hillel's view of the Law notwithstanding, most Pharisees seem to have been rigorously committed to the idea that the Law should have a place "in our kitchens, in our pockets, and in our bedrooms."

Luke suggests that Gamaliel was Paul's teacher. He has Paul tell the crowd in Jerusalem that he was "brought up in this city at the feet of Gamaliel, educated strictly according our ancestral law, being zealous for God, just as all of you are today" (Acts 22:3). Paul himself never mentions Gamaliel, and we have no way of knowing whether this speech in Acts is simply another of Luke's literary devices. But when Paul writes about this period of his life he sounds very much the school grind, teacher's pet, and all round prig: "I advanced in Judaism beyond many among my people of the same age, for I was far more zealous for the traditions of my ancestors," he tells the Galatians (Gal 1:14). The internal evidence of both Acts and the letters suggests that Paul may if anything have been more hard-line than the great Pharisee master.

The Gamaliel who emerges from the Acts is both shrewd and humane. His response to the arrest of Peter and his fellow apostles for preaching in the Temple is telling. Luke has this band of troublemakers "performing their signs and wonders" in the Portico of Solomon, one of the entrances to that magnificently cloistered outer courtyard of the Temple (Acts 5:12). It is difficult to imagine anything more provocative; on the face of it sounds like Jehovah's Witnesses buttonholing people in St. Peter's Square. When they are brought before the Sanhedrin (the council that ran the Temple and indeed was responsible for internal Jewish affairs in Judea generally) Peter's defiance produces a predictable response: "they were enraged and wanted to kill him." But Gamaliel, pointedly introduced as "a teacher of the law, respected by all the people," intervenes by suggesting that Jesus

Paul the Jew

may simply be the latest in a long line of recent troublemakers who have come and gone:

> Fellow Israelites, consider carefully what you propose to do to these men. For some time ago Theudas rose up, claiming to be somebody, and a number of men, about four hundred, joined him; but he was killed, and all who followed him were dispersed and disappeared. After him Judas the Galilean rose up at the time of the census and got people to follow him; he also perished, and all who followed him were scattered. So in the present case, I tell you, keep away from these men and let them alone; because if this plan or this undertaking is of human origin, it will fail; but if it is of God, you will not be able to overthrow them—in that case you may even be found fighting against God! (Acts 5:35–39)

The members of the Sanhedrin are convinced, and the apostles are given a good flogging and sent on their way.

The most striking thing about this passage is that there is no suggestion that Peter and the apostles are operating outside the Jewish faith; they are treated simply as another Jewish sect that may or may not flourish. Indeed there is nothing in what Peter says to the Sanhedrin to indicate that he thinks of himself as part of a separate religion either. He speaks as one addressing his co-religionists in a language they would understand: "The God of our ancestors raised up Jesus," he tells the council, and he talks of Jesus' mission to "give repentance to Israel and forgiveness of sins" (Acts 5:30–31). If you called Peter a "Christian" at this point he would probably not have understood what you meant—he was a Jew, preaching within the Jewish tradition. Christianity had not yet been born.

The way the Sanhedrin treat the apostles at this stage suggests they regarded them as fractious members of their own family, not members of a distinct religion, and that is echoed in the way the Jewish historian Josephus writes about Jesus and his followers. Many scholars believe Josephus's original words were tampered with by later generations of Christian editors, but in the text we have he speaks of Jesus as a "wise man," who rose from the dead "as the divine prophets had foretold." He does use the word *Christians,* but with none of the animus that was to characterize relations between Christianity and Judaism later; writing toward the end of the first century (his *Antiquities of the Jews* was first published in AD 93), he simply reports that "the tribe of Christians are not extinct at this day."

And yet immediately after Gamaliel's display of intelligent tolerance, Luke introduces Stephen and the story of his stoning. Why was Stephen martyred when St. Peter merited no more than a flogging?

Stephen's story is at once enigmatic and illuminating. It begins with one of those very rare admissions by Luke of division within the early church—between the "Hellenists" and the "Hebrews." It seems the Hellenists' widows were not being properly looked after, and they felt that the Hebrews' dependents were getting a better deal. It is impossible to say very much about who these Hellenists were, but it seems reasonable to assume that they were Greek-speaking Jews of the Diaspora while the Hebrews were Aramaic-speaking Jews of Judea, and there is a hint here of a distinction that foreshadows the later tensions between Jewish and Gentile Christians. Stephen, along with six others, was appointed to look after the Hellenists' interests—these seven "deacons" were effectively the church's first board of charitable trustees.

Stephen clearly relished the opportunity for leadership, and, like Peter, "did great wonders and signs among the people" (Acts 6:8). But things suddenly turned nasty. In the Acts of the Apostles it all goes wrong within the space of a paragraph. One moment Stephen is engaged in robust debate in a synagogue, the next he is up before the high priest accused of blasphemy. The charge against him is that he has been speaking "against this holy place [the Temple] and the law" (Acts 6:13)—in other words, that he had challenged the very things that made first-century Judaism what it was.

The speech Luke gives Stephen in response must surely belong to a historical convention that would have been familiar to contemporaries of the author of Acts: classical Greek historians considered it perfectly acceptable to give their principal characters polished orations that were thought to reflect their views and, more importantly, to justify the place they came to occupy in history (even if that happened as a result of events that occurred later in their careers). Stephen's speech—and this is why it is so important to an understanding of St. Paul's later career—is a clear delineation of the battle lines between Judaism and the beliefs that will eventually be known as Christianity.

It is immensely long—most of chapter 7 of the Acts of the Apostles, and around three times the length of Paul's moving and ominous farewell to the leaders of his church in Ephesus in chapter 20. It consists of an epic lesson in Jewish history, with special emphasis on God's generosity and the repeated perfidy of the Jewish people. And its climax is an attack on precisely those central facts of Jewish life that his opponents have hauled him up for threatening, the Temple and the Law. In an echo of Solomon's speech when the Temple was declared open, Stephen says:

Yet the Most High does not dwell in houses made with
human hands; as the prophet says,
  "Heaven is my throne,
      and the earth is my footstool.
What kind of house will you build for me, says
      the Lord,
      or what is the place of my rest?
Did not my hand make all these things?"
(Acts 7:48–50)

And Stephen's final insult to the Sanhedrin hints at the revolutionary ideas that will be at the heart of Paul's preaching: "You stiff-necked people," he says, *uncircumcised in heart and ears,* you are forever opposing the Holy Spirit, just as our ancestors used to do" (Acts 7:51, my italics). Circumcision was and is at the heart of the Jewish idea that the rituals of the Law are the architecture for framing humankind's relationship with God, so with Stephen's speech the idea of Law as a metaphor for that relationship is born. The first step toward breaking up the Jewish family has now been taken, and the opening salvo in what will soon become St. Paul's war has been fired—and there he is watching it from the wrong side of the barricades.

There is an intriguing phrase in Luke's account of the persecution of the church that followed Stephen's stoning: "all, *except the apostles*," he writes, "were scattered throughout the countryside of Judea and Samaria" by the crackdown instigated by Paul and his friends (Acts 8:1, my italics). Why on earth were the apostles excluded from the general roundup? How did Peter and James—already prominent figures—and the others escape the attentions of the Temple police? This could be the key to understanding the contrast between the relatively mild treatment of Peter when he was called before the Sanhedrin and the altogether more brutal punishment imposed on Stephen. Acts has given us a hint of a division within the ranks of the church between Hellenists and Hebrews. It seems likely that there was already an argument among the followers of Jesus between those like Peter, who saw themselves as remaining within the Jewish tradition, and those like Stephen, who believed they were onto to something bigger and more radical. If that was the case it would have made perfect sense for the Temple authorities to tolerate one faction while persecuting the other. And it would throw up a nice irony: Peter and Paul would at this pre-Christian stage have been pretty much on the same side of the argument, both convinced of the importance of maintaining respect for the Law and Jewish tradition.

3

Paul the Convert

The church at the point where St. Paul is said to have had his vision on the road to Damascus—"The St. Paul Vision Patriarchal Abbey," as it proclaims itself in Arabic and English on the arched gateway—is disappointingly modern; it is a round building—perfectly pleasant in design—and the whitewashed interior is hung with copies of icons. But it somehow seems an inadequate memorial to the momentous event that is supposed to have happened here.

The place itself, however, is truly numinous; it is one of those spots where you feel it might be worth listening carefully for a moment or two, just in case you pick up a hint of something more than human borne upon the breeze. It is set well back from the main road, and the sounds of modern life are muted by the immensity of the plain. The day I went there the sky was a milky blue, and to the southwest I could make out Mount Hermon under a covering of snow; the Golan Heights are on its lower slopes, a reminder that because of the continuing conflict between Syria and Israel ("Occupied Palestine," as the Syrians still insist on calling it) the journey St. Paul made from Jerusalem to Damascus is impossible today. It was winter, and a line of brown, barren-looking hills led the eye down to Damascus itself.

The city was built round an oasis, and it has been there for somewhere between five and six thousand years—it has a claim to be the oldest continuously inhabited city in the world. This is the point from which you would get your first view of it if you were travelling from Jerusalem on foot or by horse, and even today, looked at from a distance, Damascus has some of the character of a desert settlement. In the Acts of the Apostles St. Luke makes a bit of a meal of telling us what he believes happened to St. Paul on this road; the story is told no less than three times. This is the first account:

> Meanwhile Saul, still breathing threats and murder against the disciples of the Lord, went to the high priest and asked him for letters to the synagogues of Damascus, so that if he found any who belonged to the Way, men or women, he might bring them bound to Jerusalem. Now as he was going along and approaching Damascus, suddenly a light from heaven flashed around him. He fell to the ground and heard a voice saying to him, "Saul, Saul, why do you persecute me?" He asked, "Who are you, Lord?" The reply came, "I am Jesus, whom you are persecuting. But get up and enter the city, and you will be told what you are to do." The men who were traveling with him stood speechless because they heard the voice but saw no one. Saul got up from the ground, and though his eyes were open, he could see nothing; so they led him by the hand and brought him into Damascus. For three days he was without sight, and neither ate nor drank. (Acts 9:1–9)

Luke says that a "disciple" called Ananias in Damascus then had a vision in which he was instructed by God to go and find Paul, blind and shattered by what had happened to him, "for he is an instrument whom I have chosen to bring my name before Gentiles and kings and before the people of Israel" (Acts 9:15). Ananias is given very clear directions about where Paul can be found—"go to the street called Straight," says God—and when he arrives at the house where Paul is being looked after he lays his hands on his head: "And immediately something like scales fell from his [Paul's] eyes, and his sight was restored" (Acts 9:18). We do not know much about Ananias—although there is a tradition in the Syrian Church that he was one of those followers of the Way who fled Jerusalem after the murder of Stephen—but he has what must surely be the unique distinction of having baptized an apostle into the Christian church.

If you follow the story of these events in Damascus itself you really do feel the Acts of the Apostles come alive as history. The "street called Straight" still exists today. A mile long, it runs—as its name suggests—Park Avenue-like through the heart of the city. In Paul's time it would have been a hundred feet wide, with a central track for chariots, horses, and camels, and a footpath on either side. Today one side leads onto a warren of crooked lanes that flow like tributaries down toward the Ummayad Mosque. This is where Damascus does its buying and selling and it comes as close as anything I have seen to a traveller's fantasy of what an exotic Eastern souk should be like. In the spice market you can find pepper from Cochin and incense from Yemen, and since it was December when I visited the city I did most of my Christmas shopping there—returning home with an extraordinary haul of silver jewelry, silk waistcoats, and daggers for small boys. Straight Street has become much narrower over the centuries—the houses on either side have crept closer to the center so that they form a long, dark alley, much of it covered with corrugated iron to keep out the sun—but as you dodge the taxis, hawkers, and young men bending beneath bales of cloth or rolled-up carpets, you can still get a sense of what this busy Nabatean trading center must have been like two thousand years ago.

Head for the quieter reaches of Straight Street toward the east gate, and you can pay a visit to one of the principal shrines for Pauline pilgrims: Ananias's house. You turn left off Straight Street just before it ends, and you find yourself in a narrow alley flanked by especially enticing-looking jewelry and antique shops with brightly colored carpets displayed along the white walls between them. The Franciscan Order has been involved with the places of pilgrimages in Damascus since the fourteenth century; they took over Ananias's house in 1820—which is why I found it in the rather unlikely care of a monk from Chicago.

What is left of first-century Damascus is about six feet below the current street level, and Brother Tom led me down some stairs to a vault of rough stones done out as a small chapel. Just off this is a tiny cell-like room with an intriguing hole in the wall at the back; tradition—that curious character who seems to perform the same function in early church history that "White House sources" do in modern politics—holds that Christians once used it as an escape route in times of persecution. Brother Tom was in little doubt about the authenticity of the place. It has, he told me, been venerated since the first century; Ananias was the first bishop of Damascus, he explained, "and St. Paul definitely came here." Of all the places you can visit on a Pauline pilgrimage, Damascus is perhaps the most evocative.

And the story of Paul's Damascene conversion is one of those suggestive narratives we seem to find perennially valuable. It has been used again and again to make sense of a particular kind of religious experience, and we routinely reach for the phrase "Damascene conversion" when we want to describe any kind of radical change of heart. Throughout the church's history it has been seminal to people's understanding of what it means to become a Christian—think of all those Renaissance paintings of Paul being struck blind by his vision—and for an illustration of the way its influence is still making itself felt in the twenty-first century you need look no further than the George Bush White House.

It is perfectly plausible to argue that President Bush would never have made it to the Oval Office without the example Luke has left for us of Paul's conversion. When he turned forty George W. Bush was the somewhat feckless son of a famous father—a heavy drinker, with a reputation on the Houston social scene for becoming obstreperous as the hours of partying wore on. But in the mid-1980s an old school friend, Don Evans, persuaded him to start attending Bible classes, and, in the words of Howard Fineman, a *Newsweek* journalist who has been following the president's career for the past fifteen years:

> For two years Bush and Evans and their partners read the clear writings of the Gentile physician Luke—Acts and then his Gospel. Two themes stood out, one spiritual, one more political; Paul's conversion on the road to Damascus, and the founding of the church. Bush, who cares little for the abstract and a great deal for people, responded to the conversion story. He liked the idea of knowing Jesus as a friend.

In 1986, Bush gave up drinking: "It was 'good-bye Jack Daniels, hello Jesus,'" according to one friend. "I would not be president today," Bush told a group of social workers in Nashville in 2003 "if I had not stopped drinking seventeen years ago."

The influence of Luke's story was not just important in the crude sense that it helped the future president free himself from the bottle; it also gave George Bush an intellectual framework for articulating and understanding his presidential mission. I was on Capitol Hill for his speech to the Joint Houses of Congress in the aftermath of the terrorist attacks of September 11, 2001, and almost everyone I spoke to that night was carried away by a sense that something profound had changed in their president. Gone were the bumbling verbal infelicities that had given us all such innocent pleasure in the past, and in their place we heard the measured tones of a man who seemed to know what history demanded of him; 9/11 gave George Bush precisely what Luke's account gives to Paul—an immediate sense of destiny, and a conviction that he understood the purpose God had called him to serve.

Generations of ordinary Christians have read the Acts of the Apostles and found similar echoes of their own experience; Luke's account of what happened on the road to Damascus has become an archetype of the very idea of conversion. Unfortunately one of the few things we can say with any degree of confidence about St. Paul's life is that it is almost certainly inaccurate. It may be the best known of all the stories about Paul that have come down to us, but St. Luke's version of Paul's conversion is, to put it politely, imaginative.

Paul's own references to the experience are distressingly few, and distinctly enigmatic. The most detailed comes in his Letter to the Galatians, which is, as we saw in the last chapter, an especially useful source of autobiographical material.

> But when God, who had set me apart before I was born and called me though his grace, was pleased to reveal his Son to me, so that I might proclaim him to the Gentiles, I did not confer with any human being, nor did I go up to Jerusalem to those who were already

apostles before me, but I went away at once into Arabia, and afterwards I returned to Damascus. (Gal 1:15–17)

It seems, firstly, that Luke may have made a mistake over where Paul's experience took place; while he places St. Paul's vision very firmly on that immortalized road to Damascus during a journey from Jerusalem, Paul himself is more ambiguous; he says he "returned" to Damascus after a period in "Arabia," which would seem to suggest that he was already based there at the time. And that ambiguity obviously places a further question mark over Luke's story of Paul being despatched to persecute Damascus' Christians by the Temple authorities.

More significant, however, is the contrast between the two accounts of what Paul did in the aftermath of his conversion experience. The Acts of the Apostles tells its very charming story of him being led, blinded by revelation, into the streets of Damascus, and there given resolution to his spiritual crisis by that early father of the church, Ananias. Paul, however, specifically says that he kept his experience very firmly to himself—"I did not confer with any human being." That suggests that much of the "color" in Luke's story—the companions who "stood speechless because they heard the voice but saw no one," for example—is just that—color. If Paul meant the Galatians to take him literally when he said that he did not speak to anyone before disappearing into Arabia, then the only source for understanding Paul's conversion is Paul himself. And we must at the very least entertain the possibility that the story of his temporary blindness was intended to be a way of expressing the nature of his experience rather than an accurate description of what happened to him.

The two further references that Paul makes to his conversion experience in the First Letter to the Corinthians are, if anything, even more unsettling. Both are what one can only describe as naked demands for proper respect. "Am I not," he asks in the first, "an apostle? Have I not seen Jesus our Lord? Are you not my work in the Lord? If I am not an apostle to others, at least I am to you; for you are the seal of my apostleship in the Lord" (1 Cor 9:1–2). Later in the same letter he lists a kind of hierarchy of

Jesus' postresurrection appearances: "he appeared to Cephas [Peter], then to the twelve. Then he appeared to more than five hundred brothers and sisters at one time, most of whom are still alive, though some have died. Then he appeared to James, then to all the apostles. Last of all, as to one untimely born, he appeared also to me" (1 Cor 15:4–8). Paul is plainly using the fact that he has received a direct revelation from God as a means to bolster his authority; it must, after all, have been a powerful status symbol in the early church. Of course it is possible that he has omitted a more detailed account of the vision itself because the story would have already been well known to his audience. But he is laying out facts in a very deliberate way in these passages in order to advance an argument. If his revelation happened in the dramatic manner St. Luke recounts, would he not have provided a little more detail to underline its authenticity? The unavoidable truth is that Paul is woefully, tantalizingly, unforgivably short on information about the event that more than any other has made him one of the great figures of world history.

That should not, however, make us ignore the fact that on certain essential points Paul and Luke do agree. Clearly Paul did have some kind of life-changing experience, and whether it happened on the road to Damascus or in Damascus itself is perhaps of no great moment. Even if Luke has, in the modern media phrase, "sexed up" the account of Paul's vision, the apostle himself explicitly says that it was indeed a vision ("Have I not seen Jesus our Lord?"). Luke's interpretation of the event as the moment when Paul was charged with the task of preaching to non-Jews is supported by the apostle's own words in the Letter to the Galatians, and Luke is absolutely right to represent it as the pivotal moment in Paul's life. Everything begins here—Paul's mission, and therefore, arguably, the foundation of the Christian church. So it is worth spending a little more time trying to pick over the nature of the experience as best we can with the help of any circumstantial evidence we can find.

We can get some insight into the way Paul thought about the world of miracles and divine apparitions in general from his lecture on the etiquette of "speaking in tongues" in the First Letter to the Corinthians. Much of his correspondence with the

Corinthians revolves around an attempt to distinguish between "true" and "false" religion—the irony that orthodoxy should become such an issue in his liberating religious message is something I shall discuss in a later chapter—and it seems that the Corinthians had asked him about what had evidently become a divisive issue among them.

The idea of the Holy Spirit reaching down and touching people directly so that they could "speak in tongues" and prophesy seems to have been well established in the early church. St. Luke, with his gift for the dramatic moment and the memorable scene, gives us this striking account of Pentecost:

> [The apostles] were all together in one place. And suddenly from heaven there came a sound like the rush of a violent wind, and it filled the entire house where they were sitting. Divided tongues, as of fire, appeared among them, and a tongue rested on each of them. All of them were filled with the Holy Spirit and began to speak in other languages, as the Spirit gave them ability. (Acts 2:1–4)

Some of Paul's Corinthians seem to have taken things too far. Unlike the apostles in Luke's account of Pentecost, the tongue speakers of Corinth were apparently talking languages no one else could recognize; the technical name for this kind of religiously inspired ecstasy is *glossolalia,* and it is a feature of some forms of charismatic Christianity today. Paul addresses the issue in the first half of chapter 12 of his First Letter to the Corinthians on "spiritual gifts." He begins in his most emollient and inclusive mode. He tells his fractious flock:

> To each is given the manifestation of the Spirit for the common good. To one is given through the Spirit the utterance of wisdom, and to another the utterance of knowledge according to the same Spirit, to another faith by the same Spirit, to another gifts of healing by the one Spirit, to another the working of miracles, to another prophecy, to another the discernment of spirits, to

another various kinds of tongues, to another the interpretation of tongues. (1 Cor 12:7–10)

It sounds like a recipe for the very worst kind of modern charismatic service, full of meaningless otherworldly noise and dodgy "healing."

But at the beginning of the next chapter, in the passage so famous as a wedding text, Paul signals that he has a more rigorous approach in mind: "If I speak in the tongues of mortals and of angels, but do not have love, I am a noisy gong or a clanging cymbal" (1 Cor 13:1). An ostentatious show of religious enthusiasm is not enough. Paul points out at some length that jabbering away under the influence of the Holy Spirit is not much help to the rest of the community if they cannot understand what you are saying. He is careful not to question the integrity of those who speak in tongues, but his message is clear: "For those who speak in a tongue do not speak to other people but to God; for nobody understands them, since they are speaking mysteries in the Spirit.... [I]f you say a blessing with the spirit, how can anyone in the position of an outsider say 'Amen' to your thanksgiving, since the outsider does not know what you are saying?" (1 Cor 14:2, 16). There is even the danger that other people might think the Christians slightly crazy if too much of this sort of thing goes on: "If, therefore, the whole church comes together and all speak in tongues, and outsiders and unbelievers enter, will they not say that you are out of your mind?" (1 Cor 14:23).

Paul cannot resist a brief but characteristic boast about his own spiritual superiority ("I thank God that I speak in tongues more than all of you," 1 Cor 14:18) but the overall thrust of this passage is a plea for the place of intellect in worship: "I would rather," he declares, "speak five words with my mind, in order to instruct others also, than ten thousand words in a tongue" (1 Cor 14:19). And he lays down guidelines for the decorous deployment of this particular practice during Christian services: "If anyone speaks in a tongue, let there be only two or at most three, and each in turn; and let one interpret. But if there is no one to interpret, let them be silent in church and speak to themselves and to God" (1 Cor 14:27–28). Paul clearly does believe in the idea of a very direct, personal experience of God, but it is equally apparent that he was suspicious of promiscuous claims of divine inspiration.

The guide who took me to the spot on the road to Damascus where Paul is supposed to have had his vision was Father Steven Griffith, at the time the Anglican parish priest for the whole of Syria. It is a job title that gloriously evokes the very British habit of treating vast tracts of the world as if they were extensions of southeast England. Father Stephen's "parish" covered one of the ancient cradles of Christianity. During its Christian heyday, before the arrival of Islam, southern Syria alone had thirty-five bishops, including two "bishops of the tent," who travelled around the desert with their nomadic dioceses.

Father Steven was almost tart in his response when I asked him how he understood St. Paul's conversion. "I never," he shot back, "call it a conversion. I always think it's this wonderful moment where he sees the risen Christ, and so it's more of a resurrection appearance." At the time, I thought the distinction was simply a showy piece of cleverness, but it is in fact perceptive and helpful.

A salient characteristic of the legacy of Luke's road to Damascus story is the idea of conversion as a sudden and dramatic reversal—an experience in which someone's character is almost changed inside out. We speak of conversion as if—to use a metaphor from photography—it is like the moment when a negative becomes a print, and the dark becomes light. But was St. Paul really so bad before his "conversion"? And was he, indeed, always so very wonderfully good after it? The more I have come to know something of the apostle's character the more I am persuaded that the use of the word *conversion,* with its implication of a 180-degree change of heart, is misleading.

Matthew Arnold, in his magisterial essay "St. Paul and Protestantism," detects more continuity than difference between the religiously minded young man who was the pre-Damascus Paul and the great apostle he later became. All of Paul's life was inspired, he argues, by the ambition he expresses in his Letter to the Romans to "discern what is the will of God" (Rom 12:2); that was what drove his early devotion to the Pharisee sect as much as it did his later devotion to Jesus. "It is not often enough remarked," he writes, "how this incomparable honesty and depth in Paul's love of righteousness is probably what chiefly explains his conversion." Like anyone who has spent a little time trying to get close to Paul, Arnold sees his capacity to hold several different ways of looking at the world in his head at once—and admires it:

> Most men have the defects, as the saying is, of their qualities. Because they are ardent and severe they have no sense for gentleness and sweetness; because they are sweet and gentle they have no sense for severity and ardour. A Puritan is a Puritan, and a man of feeling is a man of feeling. But with Paul the very same fullness of moral nature which made him an ardent Pharisee, "as concerning zeal, persecuting the church, touching the righteousness which is the law, blameless," was so large that it carried him out of Pharisaism and beyond it, when he found how much needed doing in him which Pharisaism could not do.

The way Paul writes about his early life as a Pharisee is often designed to stress his youthful priggishness, and, like Luke, he uses rhetorical devices to bring home the fact that he has made such a long religious journey. But, as we shall see in a later chapter, when he writes in more detail and more reflectively about the religion of his youth in the Letter to the Romans, the longest and most mature of all his epistles, a rather more nuanced picture of his attitude to Judaism emerges. It is not so much that he has rejected it with relish, rather that he has somewhat reluctantly found himself compelled to leave it behind.

Equally there are passages in the letters that suggest Paul kept some of the least attractive qualities of his youth *after* his Damascene moment. They are most clearly revealed in his attitude to excommunication. Exclusion from the community of believers would have been a powerful sanction, for both religious and social reasons—to be shunned by a culture that set great store by solidarity and fellowship must have been a very traumatic experience. But that is exactly what St. Paul prescribes for those who break the rules. "I am writing to you not to associate with anyone who bears the name of brother or sister," he tells the Corinthians, "who is sexually immoral or greedy, or is an idolater, reviler, drunkard, or robber. Do not eat with such a one.... 'Drive out the wicked person from among you'" (1 Cor 5:11–13). His response to the shocking news that one of their number is living with his father's wife is unforgiving:

> For though absent in body, I am present in spirit; and as if present I have already pronounced judgment in the name of the Lord Jesus on the man who has done such a thing. When you are assembled, and my spirit is present with the power of our Lord Jesus, you are to hand this man over to Satan for the destruction of the flesh, so that his spirit may be saved on the day of the Lord. (1 Cor 5:3–5)

This is the old sectarian Paul speaking—the one who believes that membership of a religious community is defined by obedience to laws.

Luke suggests that the impact of Paul's vision was immediate; as soon as he had been baptized and welcomed into the church "he began to proclaim Jesus in the synagogues, saying, 'He is the Son of God'" (Acts 9:20). And after famously escaping from Damascus by being lowered over the walls in a basket (even his most enthusiastic Damascene fans are rather tentative about the tradition that identifies the place in the city where this is supposed to have happened), he goes to Jerusalem and tries to join the disciples—unsuccessfully at first, because they are too frightened by his past reputation. But even the fragment of an account that Paul himself gives us in his Letter to the Galatians suggests something more like a process of change than an instant transformation. He is absolutely clear about the facts; he did not speak to anyone in the immediate aftermath of revelation, he did not visit the apostles in Jerusalem, and he "went away at once into Arabia." It was not until three years later, Paul says, that he visited Jerusalem, and then he only spoke to Peter and James and avoided the other apostles.

Paul the Convert

What he did during those three years is and will always remain a mystery. The Acts of the Apostles itself acknowledges a period when he disappears mysteriously from the scene, and we simply have no direct evidence whatsoever of what happened to Paul between his revelation and the beginning of his mission to the Gentiles. The theory I find most attractive is that he retreated from the world for a while to digest and reflect upon the momentous nature of what was clearly an overwhelming experience, emerging only once he had satisfied himself that he understood its true meaning. Even Sir William Ramsay acknowledges that Paul may at first have been "not fully conscious of the full meaning of his mission; he was still bound by the fetters of Judaic consistency, and acted as if the door of the synagogue was the portal through which the Nations must find their way into the Church."

The rather more complex picture of Paul's conversion we get by focusing on what he tell us himself, and reading around the subject in his writing as a whole, makes it much easier to distinguish his experience from that of the kind of "born-again" Christian who prompted the journalist Catherine Whitehorn to ask, "Why do born again people so often make you wish they had never been born the first time?" I spent some time making a radio program about modern missionaries in Guatemala and met one who claimed he had been suddenly converted one night in the jungle during the Vietnam War ("it was like having real thick oil poured over my body") and now chatted regularly with God about Latin American politics, and another who said that God had told him to buy up a television channel to found a Christian broadcasting station. The distinction between that kind of thing and Paul's experience is much clearer when we manage to get behind the version of events left by Luke.

It also provides a shortcut round the argument over whether there could be a scientific explanation for Luke's account of Paul's blinding vision. The idea that the apostle suffered from epilepsy keeps cropping up in modern accounts of his life (for reasons I shall discuss in a later chapter), and a great deal of energy has been spent trying to match Luke's description of Paul's Damascene moment with the symptoms of an epileptic fit. But once you see Paul's conversion as a process, rather than hanging everything on

59

that single moment, this particular avenue of investigation becomes a harmless—although inevitably fruitless—diversion.

However, we are of course left with the second part of Father Stephen's verdict on Paul's Damascene moment, that it was a "resurrection experience." What does that mean? When Paul writes of having "seen" Jesus, is he telling us that he saw him as a living and breathing human being? Did he dream about him? Or did he simply use him as a metaphor for expressing the extraordinarily powerful religious insight that was to dominate the next two thousand years of human history?

Paul writes that "even though we once knew Christ from a human point of view, we know him no longer in that way" (2 Cor 5:16). It is sometimes suggested that this is evidence for the case that Paul and Jesus encountered one another during Paul's time as a young Pharisee in Jerusalem. The dates can be made to fit, but common sense would surely dictate that Paul would have made more in his writings of an encounter with someone he believed to be the Son of God and the Savior of humankind. Another interpretation of this passage is that Paul was no more than a religious charlatan who was prepared to claim supernatural but bogus experiences to impress his authority on members of his cult; but that suggests a degree of calculating cynicism that does not square with the passionate Paul who speaks to us from his letters. Perhaps when he says "we," he simply means the community of believers in general. Or perhaps he is referring to a visionary experience that he does not need to describe because he had so often spoken about it in person during his time with the Corinthian Christians.

If St. Paul is making it all up, he is at the very least consistent in his deceit. "The gospel that was proclaimed by me," he tells the Galatians, "is not of human origin; for I did not receive it from a human source, nor was I taught it, but I received it through a revelation of Jesus Christ" (Gal 1:11–12). Paul's letters contain curiously little of the Jesus teachings we read in the four gospels, but the presence of Christ permeates almost everything he writes. Run your eye down any page of Paul and the words *Christ* and *Jesus* leap out at you again and again. Most of us will in the end make up our own minds about Paul's Damascene experience according to our intellectual frame of reference. Many committed Christians—though not all—will accept it as a literal vision of the risen Christ. Others will choose to see it as—to a greater or lesser extent—a vivid metaphor used to illuminate the dramatic development in Paul's understanding of the meaning of religion.

It is perhaps a little fanciful, but I find an oblique reflection of the nature of Paul's experience of Jesus in his literary style. The poet Tom Paulin, who is an unreconstructed fan of Paul's way with words, says, "It is all done with images," and he puts Paul's particular literary genius down to that "extraordinary Hebrew capacity to put things down as images, to put forward ideas as images." Reflect for a moment on a few of the many really striking phrases that St. Paul has left us—I am quoting the old King James Version of the Bible here, because it does this kind of thing so much better: "O death, where is thy sting? O grave, where is thy victory?" (1 Cor 15:55); "The wages of sin is death"(Rom 6:23); "For now we see through a glass, darkly" (1 Cor 13:12); "Whatsoever a man soweth, that shall he also reap" (Gal 6:7); "The peace of God, which passeth all understanding" (Phil 4:7). These are still part of our everyday linguistic landscape, and they were minted by a poet with a gift for the alchemy that makes the abstract concrete. Perhaps the closest we can come to understanding Paul's revelation experience is to think of it as something akin to the moment when a poet makes a new metaphor.

One of the reasons that Luke's account is so popular is that his story is so much more straightforward; Christ appears, wizard-like, and works his magic, and the great dramas of Paul's life and the founding of the church are under way. But if we sum up what we do and do not know about Paul's Damascene moment we cannot, with the best will in the world, accept the simplicity of the account in the Acts of the Apostles, however dramatically satisfying it may be. It probably did not happen on the road to Damascus, it did not immediately turn Paul into a Christian, neither did it transform him from a very bad man into a very good one. There is, however, one point on which everyone agrees—St. Luke, St. Paul, and, happily, the Anglican parish priest of Syria too; when God revealed himself to Paul he gave him the task of taking his new faith beyond the Jewish community to a world audience. Indeed Paul is quite precise about the fact that this was the purpose of the revelation; God, he writes, "was pleased to reveal his son to me, so that I might proclaim him among the Gentiles" (Gal 1:16). And because of the momentous consequences of that, Paul's revelation deserves its reputation as a history-changing moment, despite all the doubts about where or how it happened. Father Stephen is by no means convinced by the road to Damascus story, but as we looked out toward Mount Hermon, across the plain St. Paul would have walked, he pointed out that a mere detail of location is irrelevant. "This," he said, "is the event that clarifies what Christianity is going to be."

4

Paul the Christian

"It was in Antioch," Luke tells us, "that the disciples were first called 'Christians'" (Acts 11:26). And Paul's part in the story of the early church in the city was decisive in shaping the religion we now call Christianity.

Paul's "lost" years end with a summons from Barnabas. A significant but elusive figure, Barnabas is generally thought to have been a Cypriot Jew who had become close to the inner circle of Jesus' followers in Jerusalem. Paul writes of him as if he were a friend and ally, and the Acts of the Apostles suggests he helped as a character witness and sponsor when the disciples expressed skepticism about the sincerity of Paul's newfound faith. Luke reports that Barnabas was sent on a fact-finding mission to the fledgling church in Antioch from the head office in Jerusalem. He was impressed by the number of converts he found, and evidently concluded that he needed help; he "went to Tarsus to look for Saul, and when he had found him, he brought him to Antioch" (Acts 11:25–26).

When St. Paul arrived in Antioch it was the third-largest city in the world after Rome and Alexandria. It had been founded by the Seleucid king Nicator I around 300 BC—the Seleucids ruled Syria and the southern half of Asia Minor—and was created capital of the Roman province of Syria by Pompey. It sounds very much like Paul's home town of Tarsus in its urban sophistication; it was the "Queen of the East," "the Beautiful and the Golden," and its citizens were "a vigorous, turbulent, and pushing race, notorious for their commercial aptitude, the licentiousness of their pleasures, and the scurrility of their wit." The writer Libanius has left us a Greek oration *In Praise of Antioch,* and although it was written well after Paul's time, it gives us the flavor of the city's life in antiquity. He describes at great length the glory of Antioch's colonnades, which he says would stretch to "a full day's march" if laid out end to end. The point of his extended architectural dissertation, he says, is that these agreeable public spaces provided an ideal environment for the chatter that was the city's life blood: "In my opinion, the most pleasant feature of cities, I would go so far as to say the most beneficial too, lies in social intercourse and association. Indeed where you have this aplenty, there you have a real city." This is café culture writ large—Pall Mall in the eighteenth century, the Left Bank of Paris in the '50s, a cross between '60s Haight-Ashbury and the West Village of today. It sounds just the sort of atmosphere in which the voluble Paul would have flourished. Quite what Jesus might have made of the city that first gave his religion a name is more difficult to say; Antioch was a mix of self-conscious chic and unabashed pagan polytheism, culturally, if not geographically, a world away from the hills of Galilee.

Libanius has given us a vivid account of the local enthusiasm for building swimming pools, which he says was encouraged by the abundance of water flowing down from the hills:

> He who has the means of laying out a new bath does so without concern about a sufficient flow of water, and has no need to fear that, when ready, it will remain dry. Therefore every district of the city carefully provides for the special elegance of its bathing establishments; these district bathing establishments are so much finer than the general ones, as they are smaller than these are, and the inhabitants of the district strive to surpass one another.

If Tarsus was a first-century New York, Antioch sounds like the Roman Empire's Beverly Hills. Just outside the city was the suburb of Daphne, a spot sacred to Apollo and Artemis: "This suburb, beautified by groves and fountains, and embellished by the Seleucids and the Romans with temples and baths, was the pleasure resort of the city, and 'Daphnic morals' became a by-word," writes H. V. Morton. Libanius can scarcely contain himself as he describes the scene: "Of Daphne there has never yet been a fitting description, nor will there ever be." But he has a shot at it nonetheless, conjuring up a visitor whose eyes are constantly drawn to new wonders: "the temple of Apollo or that of Zeus, the Olympic stadium, a perfectly delightful theater, a thick mass of cypresses, with shady paths, harmonious bird song, a gentle breeze, and odors sweeter than incense, imposing hotels, vines clinging to the walls of the halls...." Antioch is now the modern Turkish city of Antakya—its tourist authorities could do with a writer of Libanius's flair.

But Antioch was also one of those cities where two worlds rubbed up against one another. The flint that ignited the first Christian spark was its substantial Jewish community—around 10 percent of the population. There had been Jews in the city since its foundation, and Seleucus Nicator gave them the same privileges as the Greeks and Macedonians who made up most of the population. Many more settled there after following Alexander the Great's all-conquering armies as traders. Antioch's relative proximity to Jerusalem made travel between these two great urban centers easy. And despite the city's love of pleasure and beauty, the powerful Hebrew creed of ethical monotheism had infected the chatter that Libanius thought so central to its charm.

Josephus tells us that the Jews "made proselytes of a great many of the Greeks perpetually, and therefore after a sort brought them to be a portion of their own body." These non-Jews who made a semiconversion to Judaism are often referred to as "God fearers" (the term used by St. Luke in the Acts of the Apostles), and although our knowledge of them is limited they cast a chink of light on the way religious ideas where changing in the first century. I am just old enough to have caught the tail end of that old-fashioned educational system that held classical culture to be the high point of civilization, and I can remember idly wondering as I sweated through my gerunds and aorists, how people who were so sophisticated in so many ways could have subscribed to quite such silly religious beliefs; if the ancient Greeks and Romans really were so far ahead of anyone before or since as writers and thinkers, surely they must have worked out the flaws in the idea that we live in a world peopled by nymphs and centaurs?

It is of course a completely anachronistic question, but it pushed itself to the forefront of my mind again more than thirty years later as I sat in the theater at Ephesus, reading Luke's account of the silversmiths' riot that Paul provoked there. At the souvenir stalls outside you can buy statuettes of the goddess who was at the root of all the trouble. They represent her with what looked to me like a quite astonishing number of breasts, falling in phalanxes from her chin to her navel—they are sometimes said to be representations of "festoons of bulls' testicles." Although she carries the name of the Greek goddess Artemis (St. Luke calls her Diana, Artemis's Roman equivalent), she is thought to be a local deity dating back at least a thousand years before St. Paul visited the city. The contrast between the crudity of the city's cult and the very advanced lifestyle you can discern even in the ruins of its architecture is striking.

The little we know of the God fearers suggests that by Paul's time there were indeed significant numbers in these glittering cities who were no longer satisfied with the old gods and goddesses, and that the phenomenon Josephus records may have been a symptom of a more general spiritual hunger that polytheism could not satisfy. Religion in the Roman Empire at this period was a curious mixture. At around the time of Christ's birth Caesar Augustus, the first emperor, encouraged worship of the traditional Roman gods and goddesses as part of his campaign to restore stability; in the countryside Faunus guarded the flocks and Saturn the crops, the Lares and Penates secured the hearth, and the showy state religion of the imperial capital—Rome had roughly as many temples then as it has churches today—centered around Jupiter and Juno. But peace, good roads, and a degree of safety on the seas allowed all sorts of cults and belief systems to swirl around the Mediterranean basin—the Great Mother from the East, Mithras from Persia, and Isis from Egypt. And of course in the outposts of the empire local gods and goddesses like the Ephesian Artemis continued to flourish; Sir William Ramsay is so shocked by the details of one form of cultic worship in Asia Minor that he almost manages to choke in print: "The Christian writers," he says, "give a terrible picture of the repulsive and amoral drama of divine life that was acted before the initiated in the

Phrygian mysteries. The details cannot be quoted." There seems to have been a good deal of incestuous sex involved, with a dose of self-mutilation thrown in.

The Jews of antiquity—unlike Jews today—were enthusiastic proselytizers for their religion. As early as 139 BC all the Jews of Rome were expelled from the city, apparently for seeking converts; the historian Valerius Maximus says their offence was to "introduce their own rites to the Romans" and that they were accused of "infecting Roman morals" with a foreign cult. In the final days of the Roman Republic and during the early empire period, Jewish proselytizers evidently found a receptive audience among those who reacted against the polytheistic and pagan free-for-all of the prevailing culture. In contrast to the magnificence of the Temple in Jerusalem, the synagogues that would have been the first point of contact for many of those intrigued by Hebrew monotheism are likely to have been modest buildings. "Anyone going through the streets of a great Hellenistic city on the Mediterranean sea-board in the days of the Emperors Augustus and Tiberius," writes Adolf Deissmann, "after he had admired the splendid marble temples of the ancient gods and of the deities more recently arrived from abroad, would also perhaps notice in one of the less pretentious quarters of the city a plainly-built place of worship without an altar. At best it had for ornament a frieze of vine-leaves or olive-branches, but otherwise it was without outward decoration, and within the walls were bare and there was no image of a god." Deissmann calls the synagogues "a silent, and, the history of religion tells us, extremely effective protest against the worship of images by the polytheistic pagans." If it was the grandeur of the idea of ethical monotheism, rather than the splendor of the buildings in which it was expressed, that fascinated these potential converts, the means for them to find out more about the Jewish faith lay readily to hand. Most Jews of the Diaspora used the Septuagint, the Greek translation of the Old Testament (it is thought to have been given its name because seventy translators worked to produce it). The Septuagint marked the intersection of the Hellenistic and Hebrew worlds, and it made possible, as Deissmann puts it, "a highly effective propaganda for the One God of the Jews among pagans who had become weary and doubtful under polytheism."

The God fearers were to be a critical factor in St. Paul's campaign to take the message of Christ to the Gentiles. And the slightly ambiguous religious no-man's-land they occupied was to provide the battlefield for the absolutely seminal conflict between him and St. Peter that blew up in Antioch. The number of God fearers who made a full conversion to Judaism seems to have been fairly small; circumcision was a very big step indeed, and at one point late in the first century the circumcision of a non-Jew was made a capital offence. That stern injunction in the Jerusalem Temple—"Let no Gentile enter within the balustrade and enclosure about the holy place and whosoever is caught let him be responsible for himself because death follows"—must surely have been a disincentive to those who sought to embrace the Jewish faith too intimately. The God fearers are more likely to have had a looser adherence to Judaism. Edith Smallwood's exhaustive history of the Jews under Roman rule has them "clinging to its [Judaism's] fringes by the adoption of monotheism, Sabbath-observance, dietary laws and the major requirements of the moral code, but shrinking from the decisive commitment of stamping themselves as Jews." It meant that in a city like Antioch, with its significant God-fearing community, the question of exactly what did and did not constitute membership in the Jewish family was likely to have been a matter of almost daily debate among those who sought refuge from the punishing sun beneath the cool elegance of the colonnades described by Libanius.

Paul was not the only agent behind the spread of the new religion around the empire; we know, for example, that there were believers in Rome itself long before he got there, although how Christianity reached the heart of the known world is one of those questions that remain tantalizingly unanswerable. In Antioch, according to the Acts of the Apostles, the first followers of the Way arrived in the wake of the crackdown that followed Stephen's martyrdom: "Now those who were scattered because of the persecution that took place over Stephen traveled as far as Phoenicia, Cyprus, and Antioch" (Acts 11:19). If we accept Luke's account here—and it seems perfectly plausible—it raises the intriguing possibility that the church where Paul cut his missionary teeth was built around precisely those people who had most reason to hate and fear him; they were refugees from the episode when he entered "house after house, dragging off both men and women."

The Stephen story gives us one other clue to the development of the church in Antioch. One of the other members of that Board of Trustees set up to look after church widows in Jerusalem is said to be "Nicolaus, a proselyte of Antioch" (Acts 6:5). That complicates things somewhat, because it could be taken to indicate that there were Gentile converts in Antioch *before* the stoning of Stephen and the subsequent persecution. However, it also reinforces the point that really matters: Antioch was a city where religious lines were becoming blurred, where non-Jews were attracted in large numbers to Jewish ideas, and where the followers of Jesus found a receptive audience. St. Luke is quite explicit about the way they took their message outside the Jewish family in a manner that never features in his account of what happened in Jerusalem. At first, he says, "they spoke the word to no one except Jews. But among them were some men of Cyprus and Cyrene who, on coming to Antioch, spoke to the Hellenists also, proclaiming the Lord Jesus. The hand of the Lord was with them, and a great number became believers and turned to the Lord" (Acts 11:19–21).

Luke suggests this development delighted the disciples in Jerusalem, but it also confronted them with the question of the "Jewishness" of their faith in a new and very pressing way. In Jerusalem followers of the Way were living in a culture that assumed obedience to the Law of the Jewish religion; simple things, like the fact that meat had been slaughtered in a kosher manner, could be taken for granted. Antioch, despite its well-established Jewish population and its tolerance toward Jewish customs, was a Greek city, so adherence to Jewish tradition was a matter of positive choice, not habit. Like the God fearers, the early Gentile Christians in Antioch—who were either drawn from their numbers or were, at the very least, their spiritual cousins—were faced with the dilemmas of religious observance on a regular basis in this gregarious city. The most basic forms of social intercourse—business lunches or dinner parties—were fraught with religious risk. Of the 341 Pharisaic rulings that are thought to have existed in Paul's time, 229 were dietary regulations; every time a group of Gentile and Jewish Christians met to eat together the differences between them would have been rubbed like raw nerves.

The basic question that St. Paul confronted in Antioch was really very simple: could people become full followers of Christ without adopting the customs required by Judaism? It was of course a question pregnant with meaning for the two thousand years of history that followed his attempt to address it, and the powerful feelings that run through Paul's own account of the debate suggest he understood how much was at stake. The central episode in the dispute appears to have been a meeting in Jerusalem that is now generally accepted as the first council of the church. Both Paul (in the Letter to the Galatians) and the Acts of the Apostles (in chapter 15) have left us what seem to be descriptions of this event, but there are very significant disparities between them. Library shelves all over the world groan with the weight of words produced in the academic effort to sort out these disparities. It has even led to a whole school of biblical criticism. In the mid-nineteenth century the German scholar Bauer invented something called "tendency criticism" on the basis of what he saw as St. Luke's tendency to play down differences among the apostles and to impose the perceptions of his own age on the events he is describing. But despite the dizzy-making details of differences in chronology and even in the cast of characters, the battle lines are clear in both versions of the story.

The trouble seems to have begun just after Paul's return to Antioch from his first missionary journey with Barnabas. A group of Jesus' followers from Judea turned up in the city and began to teach that only those who had been "circumcised according to the custom of Moses" could be saved. This was of course completely contrary to Paul's view, and even Luke, who hates having to report disagreement in the early church, is forced to admit that "Paul and Barnabas had no small dissension and debate with them." It was agreed that the only way to settle the question was to send a delegation to headquarters, and "Paul and Barnabas and some others" set off for Jerusalem (Acts 15:1–2). Importantly, Paul's account of the mission suggests the delegation included a representative of Antioch's Gentile Christians; he says he took

Titus with him, and remarks that he "was not compelled to be circumcised, though he was a Greek" (Gal 2:3).

Paul's main opponents in Jerusalem seem to have been his former soul mates: Pharisees who had become followers of the Way, but still insisted that recruits from outside the Jewish family must be "circumcised and ordered to keep the law of Moses" (Acts 15:5). The description of the debate among the senior management of the church that followed is so long and detailed in the Acts of the Apostles that one writer has remarked that "one is inclined to think that the author of this book of the Bible had access to the minutes of the meeting." In the end Luke reports a compromise that comes with the authority of "Jesus' brother" James. Gentile converts, James rules, will only have to take on a sort of Torah-lite: "I have reached the decision that we should not trouble those Gentiles who are turning to God, but we should write to them to abstain only from those things polluted by idols and from fornication and from whatever has been strangled and from blood" (Acts 15:19–20). A letter—the first of so many encyclicals that in later centuries would flow from the center to the church in the world—was duly dispatched to Antioch with Barnabas and Paul.

Paul's account of the outcome of the council suggests an altogether more enthusiastic endorsement of his position by the troika who formed the church's leadership in Jerusalem: "when James and Cephas [Peter] and John, who were acknowledged pillars, recognized the grace that had been given to me, they gave to Barnabas and me the right hand of fellowship, agreeing that we should go to the Gentiles and they to the circumcised" (Gal 2:9). It is striking that although Paul wants to emphasize that the blessing on his mission comes from the very top of the church, he is not willing to concede that the troika have any real authority over him; they are simply recognizing and endorsing the task he has been given by God. As he tells it, the final deal struck at the Jerusalem Council is a divvying up of missionary activity between equals—a compromise perhaps, but rather different from the one reported in the Acts of the Apostles.

But the most striking difference between the two accounts of the events surrounding the council lies in the way they present the role of St. Peter. The Acts of the Apostles has already prepared the reader for the idea that Peter was enthusiastic about seeking converts among the Gentiles with the story of Cornelius, the first full account of a non-Jew becoming a follower of Jesus. We are told that Peter baptized this God-fearing Roman centurion and his household after a vision in which God lifted the prohibition against Jews associating with Gentiles. Even so, the tone of Peter's address to the council is so "Pauline" that you cannot help wondering for a moment or two whether Luke simply got their names mixed up: "My brothers, you know that in the early days God made a choice among you, that I should be the one through whom the Gentiles would hear the message of the good news and become believers. And God, who knows the human heart, testified to them by giving them the Holy Spirit, just as he did us; and in cleansing their hearts by faith he has made no distinction between them and us" (Acts 15:7–9). In Luke's version of events, Peter emerges as an ally standing foursquare behind Paul.

But in the Letter to the Galatians Paul describes a row with Peter that paints a very different picture indeed. The passage deserves to be quoted at some length because it is, apart from anything else, a very remarkable historical document—a firsthand account of a direct conversation between the two founding saints of the Christian church.

> But when Cephas came to Antioch, I opposed him to his face, because he stood self-condemned; for until certain people came from James, he used to eat with the Gentiles. But after they came, he drew back and kept himself separate for fear of the circumcision faction. And the other Jews joined him in this hypocrisy, so that even Barnabas was led astray by their hypocrisy. But when I saw that they were not acting consistently with the truth of the gospel, I said to Cephas before them all, "If you, though a Jew, live like a Gentile and not like a Jew, how can you compel the Gentiles to live like Jews." (Gal 2:11–14)

The way this fits with the chronology of the Council of Jerusalem is one of those issues that has taken scholars round in circles for centuries. It would be convenient if the "certain people" who came from James were the "certain individuals" who "came down from Judea" in the Acts of the Apostles; that would make Paul's argument with Peter the event that precipitated the council in Jerusalem, and thus led to a general agreement on church policy. But the way the Letter to the Galatians is constructed suggests that it happened *after* the council. That would mean that both Peter and James were guilty of trying to go back on the agreement reached there, and that James actively sought to stir up trouble for Paul by sending his agents down to Antioch, even though the two men had debated and apparently already settled the central issues face to face. Seen in this light the agreement at the Jerusalem Council looks a little like the UN resolution that preceded the American and British invasion of Iraq, a deal that is initially heralded as a mark of unity, but falls apart as soon as it comes under pressure because everyone thinks it means something different.

Paul certainly uses some very undiplomatic language here; the fact that he called the first pope a hypocrite scarcely squares with the picture most of us have of relations between these two towering figures of early Christianity. And the shock he clearly felt at Barnabas's betrayal is still palpable, even though this letter was written some time after the events it describes. For all St. Luke's efforts in the Acts of the Apostles to play down the differences in the early church, there is no escaping the fact that the birth of Christianity was marked by an absolutely steaming row between St. Paul and St. Peter. And Paul was spectacularly right; had he not "opposed him [Peter] to his face" there might be no Christian church. The followers of Jesus could have simply faded away, joining the list of lost sects in Gamaliel's speech to the Sanhedrin when they were weighing up their response to the latest group of troublemakers operating in the Temple precincts.

I asked Father Scott Brodeur, the Professor of Pauline Theology at the Roman Catholic Gregorian University in Rome, how he felt about this, and he gave me a wry smile: "I hold the chair of Pauline theology," he said, "there is no chair of Petrine theology." It is no great surprise to find the episode in Antioch being used to cast doubt on the validity of Catholic claims for the office of pope. C. J. Den Heyer, who is Professor of the New Testament at the Theological University of the Reformed Churches in the Netherlands, quotes the passage in Matthew's Gospel in which Jesus praises Peter as the "rock" upon which he will build his church, and tells him, "I will give you the keys of the kingdom of heaven, and whatever you bind on earth will be bound in heaven, and whatever you loose on earth will be loosed in heaven" (Matt 16:18–19). "These words of praise cannot be applied to Peter's actions in Antioch," is his verdict. "There he was no rock." Den Heyer concludes that the famous passage on which papal authority rests was probably inserted in the Gospel at a later date.

In both the Acts and the letters Peter fades from the scene after the Jerusalem Council and the dispute in Antioch, but the argument about the Jewish Law is far from over at this stage. In the chapter of Acts that immediately follows the account of the council we are told that Paul himself arranged for a tactical circumcision; he recruits Timothy, who had a Jewish mother and a Greek father, and before they set off for new missionary fields Paul "had him circumcised because of the Jews who were in those places" (Acts 16:3). Most of the disputes that prompt passages of invective in his letters are tied up with the question of Law at some level or other, and it plays a central part in many of his affrays and scrapes as they are recorded in Acts, right up to his final arrest in Jerusalem.

The argument with Peter is also the moment of fission that triggers the intellectual nuclear explosion that is Paul's theology. You have to ask why it was that Paul won his battle with Peter; Paul's constant protestations about the strength of his claim to apostleship suggest that it was regularly questioned by his opponents, while Peter seems to have been generally acknowledged as a heavy hitter who had been close to Jesus in life. So it was certainly not status that won the day for Paul. The only plausible answer is that Paul emerged as victor simply because his case was more powerful and more appealing. The bones of all the big ideas that he develops in his Letter to the Romans are already there in his Letter to the Galatians. Immediately after his account of the way he ticked off Peter he explains his stand like this:

> We ourselves are Jews by birth and not Gentile sinners;
> yet we know that a person is justified not by the works
> of the law but through faith in Jesus Christ. And we
> have come to believe in Christ Jesus, so that we might
> be justified by faith in Christ, and not by doing the
> works of the law, because no one will be justified by the
> works of the law. (Gal 2:15–16)

The rather technical-sounding concept of "justification by faith" has lead to all sorts of arcane—and usually divisive—theological arguments. But the brilliantly simple concept behind it is perhaps Paul's single most significant contribution to the history of thought: true faith is defined by what happens in the heart and in the head, not by rules and regulations.

Then there is that extraordinarily vivid and almost mystical use of the crucifixion that will become such a leitmotiv of his writing: "I have been crucified with Christ; and it is no longer I who live, but it is Christ who lives in me. And the life I now live in the flesh I live by faith in the Son of God, who loved me and gave himself for me" (Gal 2:19–20). In Paul's writing the crucifixion is both a reality and a metaphor, and the way he explores its meaning has had enduring appeal.

Finally, a little further on in the Letter to the Galatians, there is one of those sublime passages where Paul seems to shake off the constraints of his time and speak to us across the centuries in a completely modern idiom. "There is no longer Jew or Greek," he declares, "there is no longer slave or free, there is no longer male and female; for all of you are one in Christ Jesus. And if you belong to Christ, you are Abraham's offspring, heir according to the promise" (Gal 3:28–29). To most of those outside the Christian and Jewish families, the dispute between Paul and Peter must have seemed obscure and largely irrelevant to the vigorous life and the great affairs of a metropolis of the Roman Empire. It was in fact the beginning of perhaps the most ambitious religious enterprise in human history—the attempt to build a system of belief that is both entirely inclusive and universal.

5

Paul the Missionary

Five times I have received from the Jews the forty lashes minus one. Three times I was beaten with rods. Once I received a stoning. Three times I was shipwrecked; for a night and a day I was adrift at sea; on frequent journeys, in danger from rivers, danger from bandits, danger from my own people, danger from Gentiles, danger in the city, danger in the wilderness, danger at sea, danger from false brothers and sisters; in toil and hardship, through many a sleepless night, hungry and thirsty, often without food, cold and naked. And, besides other things, I am under daily pressure because of my anxiety for all the churches. (2 Cor 11:24–28)

I find the final sentence in this famous passage of self-dramatization the most touching. It reveals the passion of the administrator (if that is not a contradiction in terms), the pride and worry of someone who has built an organization and is constantly concerned about its institutional health. Anyone who has worked in a big company will be familiar with the boss who becomes exasperated because he feels the workforce do not appreciate the hours he lavishes on the well-being of the business, and that is the Paul who addresses his followers in Corinth here.

Even Paul's fiercest enemies surely cannot deny his extraordinary energy. It has been estimated that he travelled some twelve thousand miles in the course of his missionary journeys, and the list of stamps he would have collected in a modern passport is long enough to make any foreign correspondent proud; he moved freely between what are now Israel, Syria, Lebanon,

Turkey, and Greece, visited the islands of Malta and Cyprus, and when he eventually wound up in Rome he was planning yet another journey, to Spain and Europe's western edge. All this despite the fact that he was not, by his own account, always in the best of health. The network of organizations he left behind became the foundation for the biggest and most enduring institution in history. You cannot contemplate his career without feeling admiration for his skills as a leader and man of action. How did he achieve so much when he apparently had so little to offer, in worldly terms anyway? What made it possible for a wandering Jewish preacher and part-time tentmaker to turn up in a city knowing no one, and leave it with a new Christian church firmly established there? The bones of the story—the official company history, if you like—can be found in the Acts of the Apostles, but as ever it is Paul's letters that provide the clues that really matter, and they give us an insight into a mind with that talent for inspiring people in a common cause that is the true hallmark of corporate leadership.

Luke's account of Paul's first missionary journey is formulaic, and it is shot through with the prejudice that disfigures the worst of his writing. It feels distant from the events themselves, as if Luke is relying heavily on hearsay. This is scarcely surprising; the journey marks the real beginning of Paul's public career, and takes place before he had achieved the stature that later drew so much attention to everything he did and said. It would be quite natural for Luke's sources to be a little sketchy about the details of his activities at this stage, and he makes up for the lack of firsthand reporting with some imaginative set pieces.

The journey begins with Barnabas taking Paul to visit his native Cyprus. Here the apostle engages in a Harry-Potterish competition in sorcery. He and Barnabas are challenged by a local Jewish wizard, Bar-Jesus or Elymas, and Paul curses him and blinds him—temporarily at least. This drama is played out in front of the Roman proconsul, Sergius Paulus, who was apparently so impressed that he converted to Christianity (Acts 13:1–12). The Paul we meet in the letters could certainly curse his enemies with flair, but I find it difficult to believe that this passionate polemicist secured his first high-profile convert through a specious and rather cruel trick.

However, Luke gives us a clear indication that he feels this episode marks an important turning point; until now he has referred to Paul by his Hebrew name, Saul. In Cyprus he becomes "Saul, also known as Paul" (Acts 13:9), and Paul he remains for the duration. Perhaps this was the moment when Paul emerged as the leader in the Paul-Barnabas missionary partnership. Equally, the change of name could be a way of placing Paul firmly outside the purely Jewish context of his early encounters with the Jesus belief; henceforth he will be very much the Roman citizen with a mission to the wider world.

The formula for the Paul missionary technique is established at his first significant stop back on the mainland of Asia Minor, in Antioch in Pisidia (this Antioch is not to be confused with the Antioch on the Orontes where Paul's row with Peter took place; King Nicator founded no fewer than fifteen Antiochs, all of them named after his father). The synagogue is his first target, and he is given the floor by the officials there and invited to put his case. The speech that Luke puts into his mouth is remarkably similar to Stephen's oration before his stoning—a potted history of the Jewish people and their relationship with God, and an exposition of Jesus' place as the climax of God's plans for humankind. The message is well received by both the Jews and the "devout converts" and "those who fear God" who are attending the synagogue, and by the following Sabbath the whole city has turned out to hear Paul speak. At this point the Jews grow jealous and attack Paul and Barnabas, provoking a riposte from the two missionaries that seems clearly designed for the Jewish people as a whole:

> It was necessary that the word of God should be spoken first to you. Since you reject it and judge yourselves to be unworthy of eternal life, we are now turning to the Gentiles. For so the Lord has commanded us, saying,
> "I have set you to be a light for the Gentiles,
> so that you may bring salvation to the ends of the earth." (Acts 13:46–47)

With that "mission statement" the foundation for the anti-Semitic tone of parts of the Acts narrative is laid. The Jews respond to the charge from Paul and Barnabas by "stirring up persecution" against them, and the missionary pair are driven from the city, shaking "the dust off their feet in protest" as they go (Acts 13:51). Events follow a similar pattern at their next stop, Iconium; again they use the synagogue as an entry point, win converts with their eloquence, and find themselves forced to flee because of Jewish troublemaking. It is the same story in Lystra, where Paul is stoned by the Jews so badly that he is left for dead. The "spin" St. Luke is putting on events at this point could not be clearer.

But within this rather unsatisfactory account there are a couple of points of intriguing detail that stand out from the pattern and have the ring of authenticity. Barnabas and Paul had taken along an assistant on their journey, "John, whose other name was Mark." He left the party when they arrived in Asia Minor after their visit to Cyprus ("John, however, left them and returned to Jerusalem," Acts 13:13), and there appears to have been some sort of row between them. When Barnabas later suggests taking John Mark on their next missionary journey, Paul refuses: "Paul decided not to take with them one who had deserted them in Pamphylia and had not accompanied them in the work" (Acts 15:38). It is very clear from Paul's letters that he could be spiky company, and this episode suggests he could bear a grudge too.

The Acts of the Apostles is silent about the source of this disagreement, but there is something odd about Paul's decision at this stage of the journey to travel inland to Antioch in Pisidia, Iconium, Lystra, and Derbe. The populous and flourishing cities along the coast of Pamphylia and Lycia offered much richer missionary pickings, and Paul's later habit of targeting hub cities that opened up wider networks through trade and transport suggests a sharp instinct for making good strategic choices. The inland trek was hard going—it took the apostles into the Taurus mountains—and dangerous. Paul himself has left us one tantalizingly incomplete clue to his reasoning. Writing to the churches he founded on this trip in his Letter to the Galatians, he says, "You know that it was because of a physical infirmity that I first announced the gospel to you; though my condition put you to the test, you did not scorn or despise me, but welcomed me as an angel of God, as Christ Jesus" (Gal 4:13–14).

The nature of the illness to which Paul refers has provided the material for endless speculation: epilepsy, depression, failing eyesight, and malaria have all had their champions. There is a certain logic to the idea that on being hit by a bout of malaria he decided to take refuge from the hot coastal plain in the fresher air of the mountains. Why, however, would malaria be regarded as a condition that "put you to the test"? Supporters of the epilepsy theory suggest that this phrase makes much more sense if Paul is referring to the distressing symptoms of an epileptic fit, and some argue that this is what drove a shocked John Mark to part company with Paul. It is an impossible question to settle, and remains one of the mysteries of a period of Paul's life that never quite comes into focus.

For me, the story of Paul's mission really comes alive when he makes his world-changing crossing from Asia Minor into Europe on his second missionary journey. After this pivotal moment it becomes much easier to relate the activities of the Paul of the Acts to the preoccupations of the Paul of the letters, and it is marked by a new immediacy and sharpness about the way Luke tells his story. Acts whisks Paul through this second journey from Antioch across Asia Minor—including his old hunting grounds of Phrygia and southern Galatia—in a couple of brisk, spare paragraphs. In Troas, on the coast just below the Hellespont, Paul has a vision in which a "man of Macedonia" pleads with him to make the short sea voyage to the continent that will become Christianity's heartland. And suddenly something odd happens. Halfway through a sentence, without any warning, St. Luke begins to talk in the first person: "When he had seen the vision, we immediately tried to cross over to Macedonia, being convinced that God had called us to proclaim the good news to them" (Acts 16:10).

The traditional interpretation of the so-called "we passages" in the Acts of the Apostles (there are four of them) is that they relate to periods when St. Luke and St. Paul were traveling together. Sir William Ramsay, that immovably enthusiastic fan of St. Luke as a historian, has him accompanying the apostle as a personal physician. Indeed in his commentary on this particular passage he goes one step further with an extravagantly elaborate theory. The introduction of a first-person pronoun, he suggests, indicates that Troas was the place at which St. Paul and St. Luke first met. And since "it is generally recognised that Luke must have had some connection with Philippi" (which is in Macedonia), and Paul had at that stage of his life no particular reason to recognize "a man of Macedonia" from his appearance, the man in the vision must, suddenly as if by magic, have been Luke himself.

It is a sobering illustration of the way an energetic scholarly mind, driven by a powerful and sincere faith, can open itself up to ridicule. The most obvious problem with the idea that the author of Acts is relating events he witnessed at firsthand when he writes in the first person is the difficulty of making the dates work, to which I referred in chapter 1; the Acts of the Apostles is now not thought to have been put together until the 80s or 90s of the first century, some forty years after Paul crossed from Troas to Macedonia and perhaps thirty years after his death. And even if you stretch things a little and imagine a Luke in his sixties remembering his early twenties when he first met Paul (not altogether impossible), you confront a whole new set of problems. If Luke traveled with Paul on the journeys covered by the "we passages" he would have spent long hours talking to him on the roads and the high seas, and he should have known his character and his life story very well indeed; that would make it even more difficult to explain the contradictions between other parts of the Acts and Paul's letters, and the complete absence of any reference to the letters in the Acts. Common sense suggests that Luke is not relating his own experience when his narrative switches into the first person, but that he is drawing on a source closer to the events themselves.

There is no doubt about the new bounce in Luke's storytelling here, and the diarylike detail stands in marked contrast to the more formulaic account of the first missionary journey. Paul landed in Europe at Neapolis (Kavalla as it is called today); I arrived there late at night, and the next morning the unexpected beauty of a Mediterranean port in winter light was so sharp it caught me by the throat; the snow had brought harmony to the chaotic jumble of buildings along the waterfront, and there was just a hint of summer pink softening the slate gray of the Aegean.

The Via Ignatia—the road on which Paul made his first European journey—lay under a dusting of white, and the grass poking up between the stones on which he once walked was stiff and crunchy with frost. It would have taken him a couple of days on foot to reach Philippi. The course of the old Roman road takes it directly into the center of the city—it is clearly visible at this point, with its six-inch thick stones, scored by the wheels of wagons and chariots—so Paul would immediately have found himself in the forum, the heart of Philippi's life, when he arrived.

The Via Ignatia was famous because it crossed the Greek peninsula, running for five hundred miles straight across Macedonia and Thrace; it linked the Aegean and Adriatic seas, and connected Rome with its eastern empire in Asia Minor. But it was only one artery in a transport network that remained unequaled for centuries. Like Hausmann's boulevards in Paris (which were given the width we enjoy so much today to make it more difficult for rioters to erect effective barricades), the road system of the Roman Empire was designed with military objectives in mind; it allowed the swift deployment of the legions on which the *Pax Romana* rested. Its engineers may not have appreciated that it also facilitated the spread of a belief system that would long outlive the march of military feet.

The Greek writer Plutarch, born a few years after Paul's death, paints an admiring picture of the transport network that allowed the apostle to cover such astonishing distances. "The roads were carried straight across the countryside. They were paved with hewn stones and bolstered underneath with masses of tight packed gravel; hollows were filled in, and torrents of ravines that cut across the route were bridged." The main thoroughfares were between twenty and thirty feet wide, with curbstones to bind the surface and deep ditches on either side for drainage. A nineteenth-century German historian, Heinrich Stephan, concluded that "Most of the realms of the Roman Empire had better connections and conditions than ever afterwards and even now." This second missionary journey of Paul's was certainly easier during the imperial period than it would be for many centuries thereafter; right up until in the 1830s Greece had no roads for vehicles at all.

Paul probably walked on most of his journeys—we have no evidence that he hired horses or mules—so it was still tough going; he would have been able to cover fifteen or twenty miles a day. However, once he had arrived at a main thoroughfare like the Via Ignatia he could at least be reasonably confident about his safety. The kind of bandits he might have faced in the Taurus Mountains on his first missionary journey would not have been tolerated by the authorities here, and as he traveled Paul would have passed milestones, those unrelentingly regular reminders that the roads were the bones of a vast political structure that embraced a hundred thousand square miles, most of the known world. The stones marked out distances from big cities in Roman miles and sometimes carried additional information such as transport regulations or points of more general interest; a milestone found at Pozanti in Eastern Turkey, for example, close to Paul's home city of Tarsus, carries an inscription recording the repair of the Via Tauri "which was dilapidated with age" by "leveling mountains, smashing rocks, widening roads for vehicles, and building bridges."

The only really unpleasant obstacle to comfortable travel was the quality of the inns available. Rich men carried their beds and tents with them—Julius Caesar even traveled with his own mosaic floors, and Nero's murderous mistress (and later wife) Poppaea insisted on bringing five hundred asses on her journeys so that she always had milk for bathing purposes on tap—but Paul is likely to have used the cheaper lodgings that provided basic bed and board. They carried signs like English pubs—"The Cock," "The Great Eagle," "The Snake," "The Wheel," and "The Olives" are all names that have come down to us—and the description we have of what it was like inside a "greasy tavern" is pretty unappetizing. They were filled with the smoke, smells, and clamor of the kitchen, and the bedding, which was stuffed with reeds rather than feathers, was "alive with fleas and bugs." Often the landlords were pimps and the kitchen maids doubled as prostitutes, which Paul must surely have found distressing. The quality of food in these inns was uncertain; the second-century Greek doctor Galen reports a case of a guest finding a human finger bone in his otherwise agreeable stew.

Today Paul would simply not be able to range around the Mediterranean basin with the freedom he enjoyed in the first century. Direct travel between Israel and Syria is of course impossible (the Syrian authorities still ask you to fill in a form stating whether you have ever visited what they insist on calling "Occupied Palestine"), as it is between Israel and today's Lebanon, which lies between Jerusalem and Antioch. Cyprus is divided by the heavily militarized Green Line, which separates the Greek and Turkish areas of the island. When Paul crossed from what is now Turkey into Greece he would be moving into a European Union that is increasingly wary about letting in those outside its borders. Quite how this peripatetic troublemaker would have fared under current immigration and asylum regulations is difficult to say.

In the first century there were no real borders anywhere within the Roman Empire, no passports or visas required; it was quite normal for students from Rome to travel to Marseilles to study, for young men from Egypt or Libya to make the journey to the imperial capital for the same purpose, or for Romans suffering from tuberculosis to be sent off to North Africa for the benefit of the air. It must have been an intoxicatingly liberating time to live; you needed little more than intellectual curiosity, stout limbs, and modest means to qualify as a world traveler. Aristides of Smyrna was one of many writers who eulogized the *Pax Romana* that has "merged all nations into one family"; Rome, he says, has "measured the earth, bridged the rivers and made roads through the mountains, peopled the deserts and ennobled all things...opened every gate and given every man his freedom, to see all things with his own eyes." Ludwig Friedlander is probably right to conclude, in his exhaustive study of daily life in the empire, that travel was more extensive during this period than it was at any time until peaceful politics and technological advances opened up Europe again in the nineteenth century.

"Europe is the Church, and the Church is Europe," declares Hilaire Belloc on the opening page of his polemical essay "Europe and the Faith." "My object in writing," he explains, "is to show that the Roman Empire never perished but was only transformed; that the Catholic Church which it accepted in its maturity caused it to survive, and was, in the origin of Europe, and has since remained, the soul of our Western civilisation." Belloc's Roman Catholic triumphalism may not be to everyone's taste, but few would deny the absolutely central role that Christianity played in the formation of European civilization. And if you walk, New Testament in hand, a short way westward beyond the main Philippi ruins, you can imagine yourself at the point where the great romance between Europe and the faith began. There's a small concrete amphitheater by the riverbank, and an island with a willow tree and a whitewashed shrine commemorating what is said to have happened here—the first recorded baptism on European soil:

> On the sabbath day we went outside the gate by the river, where we supposed there was a place of prayer; and we sat down and spoke to the women who had gathered there. A certain woman named Lydia, a worshiper of God, was listening to us; she was from the city of Thyatira and a dealer in purple cloth. The Lord opened her heart to listen eagerly to what was said by Paul. When she and her household were baptized, she urged us, saying, "If you have judged me to be faithful to the Lord, come and stay at my home." And she prevailed upon us. (Acts 16:13–15)

The Greek Orthodox Church has built a modest chapel and a baptistery close by; the amphitheater by the riverbank is there for christening parties, and there are a couple of steps leading down to the water for those who want to go for baptism by total immersion. It is a charming spot, and it is easy to see the appeal of a christening here. But when I visited it with Dr. Samuel Provost, a French archaeologist who devotes his life to digging up Philippi's past, I found him distinctly sniffy about the whole enterprise. The only archaeological evidence he has found indicates that it was a cemetery, and there is no sign of the "place of prayer," presumably a synagogue, mentioned in the Acts of the Apostles. The area does definitely have a place in history, and a very significant one; it was where the Roman Republic died. Lydia's shrine stands slap bang in the middle of the battlefield on which Octavius and Antony defeated Brutus and Cassius nearly a hundred years before Paul's visit. But the tradition that places the baptism of Lydia here is very recent. In the late nineteenth and early twentieth century, the Greek government went in for a wholesale renaming program as part of a propaganda campaign; they were trying to encourage a sense of Greek identity and to banish the memory of Ottoman rule, and whenever they could they chose names that evoked the country's classical or Christian past. So the small village that had grown up near Philippi's ruins was given the name Lydia. Not for the first time on this journey, I found that as you peel back the layers of history the past can become more, not less confusing, and you are liable to find the truth being spun at every stage.

But Lydia herself somehow stands above these muddy waters. She is such an unlikely figure to be given the prominent role she has in the development of Christianity that you feel she must be real. She is, firstly and most obviously, a woman, and, furthermore, a woman of means. There is evidence that women of the empire period were slightly more liberated than we might think; the ruins of Pompeii have thrown up records of a number of rich business-women who sponsored public building projects, for example. But this was still very much a patriarchal society in which, to use Paul's own words, "the husband is the head of the wife," and women of Lydia's independent status were something of a rarity. Whether or not Paul deserves his reputation as a misogynist is a question I shall come back to in a later chapter, but it is certainly striking that he chooses to begin his evangelizing work at this critical juncture of his missionary journey by targeting a woman. On the face of it, fur-thermore, she does not seem to have been the sort of woman who would naturally appeal to him. Lydia was in the fashion business; Thyatira was famous for its dyers, and purple, extracted from the murex shellfish, was very much a luxury item. We do not know very much about Paul's attitude to fashion, but I cannot imagine he approved of it very much. The advice he gives the pleasure-lov-ing Corinthians on personal grooming is stern ("any woman who prays or prophesies with her head unveiled disgraces her head," 1 Cor 11:5) and deeply conventional ("Does not nature itself teach you that if a man wears long hair, it is degrading to him, but if a woman has long hair, it is her glory?" 1 Cor 11:14–15). He was clearly not the sort of man who would naturally settle down for a good chat about the latest line in toga toggles. Finally, unlike most of those in the anonymous crowds Paul preached to in Asia Minor, Lydia is a Gentile.

All of these factors distinguish the conversion of Lydia from the proselytizing formula Paul follows in the account of that first missionary journey. It may of course have been that Lydia simply listened to Paul preaching and pressed her attention on him—that she chose him rather than the other way round. But Paul has left us a slightly chilling picture of the calculating way he went about finding converts:

> I have made myself a slave to all, so that I might win more of them. To the Jews I became as a Jew, in order to win Jews. To those under the law I became as one under the law (though I myself am not under the law) so that I might win those under the law. To those outside the law I became as one outside the law (though I am not free from God's law but am under Christ's law) so that I might win those outside the law. To the weak I became weak, so that I might win the weak. I have become all things to all people, that I might by all means save some. I do it all for the sake of the gospel, so that I may share in its blessings. (1 Cor 9:19–23)

Political commentators often remark that the capacity to leave everyone feeling that you understand and share their views and values is a great political gift that can sometimes make it possible to reconcile apparently irreconcilable positions. Most of us, I suspect, find it a little creepy, but Paul seems to glory in the skills of social insincerity, so long as they are deployed in a greater cause. There must surely be a very good chance that he chose to focus his attention on Lydia for sound strategic reasons.

It certainly did not hurt that she was rich. Faced with the alternative of more nights in the local Snake or Wheel Inn, the offer of a bed in the home of a successful businesswoman in the luxury goods trade must have been welcome even to the austere

Paul. More importantly, though, her invitation gave him the chance to establish a base of operations and provide a meeting place for newly converted Christians in the city. Lydia was converted with her "household," and a household meant much more than a modern nuclear family; it would have included slaves, hired laborers, perhaps also tenants and business associates and more distant kinsmen as well. In general the members of a household would have been expected to follow the example of its head, so when Paul converted Lydia's household or, later on this missionary journey, the synagogue official called Crispus "together with all his household," it is reasonable to assume that a substantial number of people were involved (Acts 18:8).

There is plenty of evidence in both the Acts of the Apostles and Paul's letters that "house churches"—like the one he would have been able to establish as a result of Lydia's hospitality—were the building blocks of his new religion. The Letter to Philemon, for example, is addressed to "Archippus our fellow soldier, and to the church in your house" (Phlm 2), and elsewhere he praises "members of the household of Stephanas" who "have devoted themselves to the service of the saints" (1 Cor 16:15). These private houses were the places where the members of the early church met, talked, ate together, and celebrated the first version of the Mass. It seems likely that the Eucharist was already a prominent part of Paul's teaching when he visited Philippi, because he taught the Corinthians about it later on the same missionary journey. In his first letter to them he writes:

> For I received from the Lord what I also handed on to you, that the Lord Jesus on the night when he was betrayed took a loaf of bread, and when he had given thanks, he broke it and said, "This is my body that is for you. Do this in remembrance of me." In the same way he took the cup also, after supper, saying, "This cup is the new covenant in my blood. Do this, as often as you drink it, in remembrance of me." For as often as you eat this bread and drink the cup, you proclaim the Lord's death until he comes. (1 Cor 11:23–26)

If Paul targeted Lydia because she had a big enough drawing room to accommodate a congregation for this most sacred celebration, who can blame him? The idea that all the first Christians were poor has a long and distinguished provenance. The second-century pagan polemicist Celsus dismissed Christianity as a religion that appealed to "the foolish, the dishonorable and stupid, and only slaves, women, and little children," and in the early twentieth century the German giant of Pauline scholarship Adolf Deissmann pictured Paul working among the "unliterary masses of the great cities." But modern scholars like Wayne Meeks paint a more complex picture: the world in which Paul operated, he argues, included "no landed aristocrats, no senators, *equites*," but it did include large numbers of the upwardly mobile middle classes; we find, he says, "probable freedmen and the descendents of freedmen, who have advanced in wealth and position, especially in the Roman colonies of Corinth and Philippi. We find wealthy artisans and traders; high in income, low in occupational prestige. We find wealthy, independent women. We find wealthy Jews."

Paul may also have been mindful of the new network of contacts Lydia opened up for him. As a Diaspora Jew he would have been all too familiar with the idea that there could be close ties between widely scattered communities, and when he turned up at the synagogues on his first missionary journey he was tapping into a cultural and religious system that linked Jews right across the empire. But when he moved into Gentile territory he needed a new set of connections to work with, especially as the Jewish network became more hostile, and closed down to him. Lydia is likely to have had access to some of the trading networks that were spreading so vigorously around the empire under the *Pax Romana*.

She could scarcely have chosen a better center for her operation. Today Philippi seems somehow stranded on the valley floor; because the Greeks have built their modern road along the course of the Via Ignatia, the old city's ruins are bisected by a strip of tarmac, and as cars whiz past the forum it looks mournful and irrelevant, left behind by the march of time. There is nothing obvious to suggest why all this ruined glory was built here. But in Paul's day Philippi was the gateway to Europe; anyone traveling from

Asia Minor to the western empire came this way. A well-established Christian church in the city might catch all sorts of passing trade, and it is perhaps not too fanciful to think of Lydia's sales reps fanning out across the Greek peninsula, bearing Paul's ideas along with their bales of gorgeous purple cloth. There is a similar example of Paul's ability to exploit alternative networks in the Acts account of the way he established himself in Corinth; he met a Jewish couple there, Aquila and Priscilla, who, like him, were tentmakers, and entered into partnership with them. These two seem to have had contacts all over the place; in Paul's letters they pop up in Ephesus and later surface back in their home city of Rome.

There is some circumstantial evidence that Paul may have taken money from Lydia. He certainly was not one of those preachers who enrich themselves by playing on the generosity of the credulous. The letters are not the work of a man who cares much about material things, and there is no reason to question Paul's reflection that "I have learned to be content with whatever I have. I know what it is to have little, and I know what it is to have plenty. In any and all circumstances I have learned the secret of being well-fed and of going hungry, of having plenty and of being in need" (Phil 4:11–12). And he was willing to work if he had to: "we worked night and day," he reminds the Thessalonians, "so that we might not burden any of you while we proclaimed to you the gospel of God" (1 Thess 2:9). But money was, inevitably, a difficult issue, and in an ill-tempered passage in his First Letter to the Corinthians Paul reminds them that he never asked them for financial help: "I robbed other churches by accepting support from them in order to serve you. And when I was with you and was in need, I did not burden anyone, for my needs were supplied by the friends who came from Macedonia" (2 Cor 11:8–9). The openhandedness of the Philippian Christians—including, presumably, Lydia—inspires a gracious thank-you note at the end of Paul's letter to the community there:

> You Philippians indeed know that in the early days of the gospel, when I left Macedonia, no church shared with me in the matter of giving and receiving, except you alone. For even when I was in Thessalonica, you

sent me help for my needs more than once. Not that I seek the gift, but I seek the profit that accumulates to your account. I have been paid in full and have more than enough; I am fully satisfied, now that I have received from Epaphroditus the gifts you sent, a fragrant offering, a sacrifice acceptable and pleasing to God. (Phil 4:15–18)

Paul's correspondence with the Philippians was some time after his first visit to the city, so if seems they went on shelling out to support him on a long-term basis.

Paul's time in Philippi unravels in an entirely characteristic manner. A slave girl who was believed to have the power of divination follows the Paul party around for "many days" declaring in a loud voice to anyone who would listen, "These men are slaves of the Most High God, who proclaim to you a way of salvation." In the end Paul simply loses his temper and, "very much annoyed, turned and said to the spirit, 'I order you in the name of Jesus Christ to come out of her'" (Acts 16:18). The slave girl's owners were enraged to lose their income from her prophecies and had Paul and his companion Silas beaten with rods and locked up for the night. In the middle of night, while Paul and Silas are singing hymns, a providential earthquake shakes open the doors of the jail. But Paul refuses to leave until he has had an apology. Only once honor is finally satisfied, does he move on down the Greek peninsula.

The next leg of Paul's second missionary journey follows a more familiar course. In Thessalonica Paul and Silas preach successfully at the synagogue, but their activities provoke a riot by the Jews, so they move swiftly on to Beroea. The Jews there are more receptive, but the Jews of Thessalonica have followed them and stir up trouble all over again. Paul is moved on to Athens by "the believers," presumably for his safety, while Silas and Timothy remain behind. Athens was a pale shadow of its former self by this stage, but it still liked to think of itself, in Milton's phrase, as a place "where books and wits were ever busier that in any other part of Greece." Luke's account of Paul's time there includes the odd episode of his speech at the Areopagus, the hill where the city's Higher Council met and its philosophers would put on public displays of intellectual virtuosity.

Paul's foray into Athenian philosophical debate is sometimes cited as an illustration of his modernity: "as I went through the city and looked carefully at the objects of your worship," he says,

> I found among them an altar with the inscription, "To an unknown god." What you therefore worship as unknown, this I proclaim to you. The God who made the world and everything in it, he who is Lord of heaven and earth, does not live in shrines made by human hands, nor is he served by human hands, as though he needed anything, since he himself gives to all mortals life and breath and all things. From one ancestor he made all nations to inhabit the whole earth, and he allotted the times of their existence and the boundaries of the places where they would live, so that they would search for God and perhaps grope for him and find him—though indeed he is not far from each one of us. For "In him we live and move and have our being," as even some of your own poets have said. (Acts 17:23–28)

This is an Oxbridge High-Table St. Paul we have not met before; familiar with classical poetry, easygoing about big ideas, curious about comparative religion, open-minded and generous spirited in his approach to paganism and the kind of generalized view of God one might define as theism. And the idea that our lives' purpose is to "grope" for God is very modern indeed. If Luke was our only source of information about Paul's life, we might believe this picture of the apostle—it seems entirely consistent with the worldview of a well-educated citizen of Tarsus.

However, we have a pretty good idea of what Paul's thinking really was during this period because his Letter to the Thessalonians (it is one of two in the biblical canon, but the second is generally agreed to be someone else's work) appears to have been written later on this same missionary journey. It is ferociously apocalyptic, with its striking and enduring metaphor of the day of the Lord coming "like a thief in the night" (1 Thess 5:2).

Paul tells the Thessalonians not to grieve for those who die before the Second Coming:

> For this we declare to you by the word of the Lord, that we who are alive, who are left until the coming of the Lord, will by no means precede those who have died. For the Lord himself, with a cry of command, with the archangel's call and with the sound of God's trumpet, will descend from heaven, and the dead in Christ will rise first. Then we who are alive, who are left, will be caught up in the clouds together with them to meet the Lord in the air; and so we will be with the Lord forever. Therefore encourage one another with these words. (1 Thess 4:15–18)

It is stirring stuff, drawing deeply on Paul's roots in Judaism; and it is extremely difficult to reconcile the archangel and the trumpet blowing with the reasoned Hellenism of the speech on an "unknown god" that is recorded in Acts. A. N. Wilson concludes that Luke's account of the speech on the Areopagus is the "strongest possible indication of the fact that Acts is a late work, belonging to a period of Christianity which post-dates Paul and his world by as much as a quarter of a century." Paul's religion was anything but logical, indeed it was shot through with paradox: "For Jews demand signs and Greeks desire wisdom, but we proclaim Christ crucified, a stumbling block to Jews and foolishness to Gentiles, but to those who are the called, both Jews and Greeks, Christ the power of God and the wisdom of God. For God's foolishness is wiser than human wisdom…" (1 Cor 1:22–25).

Driven by that apocalyptic vision of a Second Coming, Paul went about his mission to the Gentiles at breakneck speed. Acts tells us that his visit to Philippi lasted "some days," and at his next main stop, Thessalonica, it took "three Sabbaths" of debate with the city's Jews before things got too hot for him and he had to be bundled out of town (although there must be some doubt about Luke's accuracy here; as we have seen, in Paul's Letter to the Thessalonians he says he worked while he was with them, which would surely suggest a longer stay). Only when he reached

Corinth did he really settle down—he seems to have spent some eighteen months in the city, and it was probably from here that he wrote to the Thessalonians. Like one of those modern entrepreneurs who is better at setting up companies than running them, he found that things got out of hand in the churches he had established, and he used his letters in the manner a senior executive uses a corporate e-mail—as a mechanism for "cascading" his message via the local line-management structures. The letters almost always have a clear practical starting point, and it usually involves trouble on the shop floor. Paul writes to the Corinthians, for example, "It has been reported to me by Chloe's people that there are quarrels among you, my brothers and sisters" (1 Cor 1:11), and then launches into his stern lecture on the dangers of divisions within the Christian community, and the Letter to the Galatians gets underway with "I am astonished that you are so quickly deserting the one who called you in the grace of Christ and are turning to a different gospel" (Gal 1:6).

The more time I spend with Paul's letters the more I appreciate the richness of the variety of ways in which they can be read. We traditionally go to them for their theology, and very vivid they are as the earliest written statement of Christian beliefs. But they can also be read as autobiography or diaries—at times they have a Peyps-like verve and frankness—travelogues and social history. And if you approach them with the astonishingly ambitious practical goals that Paul set himself in mind, it is like opening a very early administrative file from some vast transnational corporation.

The first real postal system had been introduced by the emperor Augustus; couriers traveled along routes carefully mapped out with staging posts for changes of horse and sleeping quarters. But the system in the first century was reserved for military and administrative directives—most private individuals had to rely on the more ad hoc expediency of finding someone traveling in the right direction and handing over a letter, presumably with fingers firmly crossed. In the busy commercial world opened up by the *Pax Romana*, that would have presented no great problem, and there is plenty of evidence of vigorous correspondence around the empire during this period; the records of a foreign doctor in Rome during the second century, for example, show him being consulted by letter from Asia, Gaul, Spain, and Thrace, and receiving parcels of medicine from Syria, Palestine, Egypt, Cappadocia, Pontus, Gaul, Spain, and Mauretania.

Paul preferred to use couriers who were part of the church's leadership structure. This helped to cement the idea of the church as a universal body, which gave its members a new network of relationships reaching beyond those of city, race, trade, and social standing that they had acquired through birth or the habits of life before conversion. The letters are full of greetings and salutations that encourage this wider sense of brotherhood; when he writes to the Corinthians for a second time, for example, Paul includes "all the saints throughout Achaia" in his opening greeting (2 Cor 1:1), and the First Letter to the Corinthians, written from Ephesus, ends with "All the brothers and sister send greetings. Greet one another with a holy kiss" (1 Cor 16:20). "The letters of the Pauline circle are rich in words and phrases that speak of Christians as a special group and of the relations between them in terms charged with emotion," Wayne Meeks observes. "Especially striking is the language that speaks of the members of the Pauline group as if they were a family." Paul is at his most attractive when he is emphasizing the ties of affection that bind the family of believers together: "we were gentle among you, like a nurse caring for her own children," he writes to the Thessalonians. "So deeply do we care for you that we are determined to share with you not only the gospel of God but also our own selves, because you have become very dear to us" (1 Thess 2:7–8).

Paul's administrative genius is in making the ideals he preaches a reality in the way his new institution operates. Through the letters he seeks to create the sense of a new community that transcends old loyalties, a practical expression of that idea so vividly expressed to the Galatians: "There is no longer Jew or Greek, there is no longer slave or free, there is no longer male and female; for all of you are one in Christ Jesus. And if you belong to Christ, you are Abraham's offspring, heir according to the promise" (Gal 3:28–29). The letters also convey the idea that membership of the new Christian network involves mutual rights and duties of hospitality. Paul asks the Romans to look after Phoebe, a "deacon of the church at Cenchreae" and to "help her in whatever she may require" (Rom 16:1–2). He makes a similar request on behalf of Timothy to the Corinthians (1 Cor 16:10–11) and he asks himself to stay with Philemon: "One thing more—prepare a guest room for me, for I am hoping through your prayers to be restored to you" (Phlm 22). I was educated at a monastic boarding school, and we were told that a Benedictine education gave us the right to enjoy Benedictine hospitality anywhere in the world; in theory we could knock on the door of any monastery, say "Filius Benedicti sum"—I am a son of Benedict—and we would get a bed for the night. In the same way, Paul's converts must have felt the thrill of being linked into a whole new network of contacts, especially in an age when the ease of travel made it really quite likely that some of them would turn up in a new city needing a bed.

Paul's personal authority within the early Christian communities he founded was naturally very powerful, and there is evidence that other people tried to exploit it by appropriating his name. As the Letter to the Galatians draws to a close, Paul makes a point of the fact that he is writing it himself (he would usually have employed a scribe): "See what large letters I make when I am writing in my own hand!" (Gal 6:11)—in other words, this is the genuine article, not a forgery. There is a similar formula at the end of the First Letter to the Corinthians, and the possibility that there were fake Paul letters floating around at a very early stage is leant weight by the Second Letter to the Thessalonians, which contains that reference to a "letter, as though from us, to the effect that the day of the Lord is already here," and ends with a very self-conscious claim to authenticity: "I, Paul, write this greeting with my own hand. This is the mark in every letter of mine; it is the way I write" (2 Thess 3:17). Ironically of course 2 Thessalonians is considered, by general scholarly consensus, to be one of those in the biblical canon that was not written by Paul himself and was probably composed after his death at the end of the first century. But it does give us a sense of the power of the Paul brand name. By the time Paul packed his bags in Corinth and set sail for Asia Minor at the end of his second missionary journey, Pauline Christianity, public limited company, had a solid foothold in the European religious marketplace.

6

Paul the Divider

Dr. Pinchas Cooper, a dentist from north London, emigrated to Israel with his family in 1990. He had found an office in a modest apartment block just outside the center of Jerusalem, and developed a new professional line; in addition to his dentistry he works as a *mohel*, the man who performs the ritual Jewish circumcision.

This is how he described the process:

> The foreskin is gripped between the thumb and the forefinger of the mohel. He then places a shield over it to prevent any accidental cutting of parts that should not be cut. The foreskin is then removed with a scalpel and the inside skin is also removed to expose the tip of the penis completely. The wound is then dressed with a sterile bandage. The diaper is replaced and when the baby is dressed again a cup of wine is poured. The mohel recites blessings over this cup of wine, following which the baby is given his name and sent back to his mother.

In Paul's time there were no sterile bandages, and the mohel cleaned the wound by taking the penis in his mouth. For male Gentile converts to the Judaism of the first century, who faced this operation as adults, it would have been extremely painful, and there was a very real risk of mutilation or infection. But that, as Dr. Cooper saw it, is part of the point; circumcision involves taking a risk for God. He pointed out that in times of pogroms and persecution circumcision also meant that Jews could be easily identified, and they were happy to carry that risk too.

It is difficult for outsiders to understand what circumcision means to Jews. Catholics perhaps find it slightly easier than most; we are familiar with the kind of rituals that make you feel at home with co-religionists anywhere in the world, like blessing yourself from the holy water font when you enter a church or genuflecting before sitting down in a pew. But circumcision is more than a ritual; it is a signature on the agreement between humanity and God. In the Book of Genesis God tells Abraham:

> This is my covenant, which you shall keep, between me and you and your offspring after you: Every male among you shall be circumcised. You shall circumcise the flesh of your foreskins, and it shall be a sign of the covenant between me and you. Throughout your generations every male among you shall be circumcised when he is eight days old, including the slave born in your house and the one bought with your money from any foreigner who is not of your offspring. Both the slave born in your house and the one bought with your money must be circumcised. So shall my covenant be in your flesh an everlasting covenant. Any uncircumcised male who is not circumcised in the flesh of his foreskin shall be cut off from his people; he has broken my covenant. (Gen 17:10-14)

God's message to Abraham could not be clearer. Circumcision is the cornerstone of Judaism. As Pinchas Cooper explains it: "The reason why we observe the commandments is first and foremost because God commanded us to do so. After that it is our obligation to try and analyze the reasons for all this and ask what we can learn from the performance of these commandments. But essentially what we would say is that what was God-given is not negotiable." Circumcision is at the top of Judaism's list of nonnegotiable items.

The Jerusalem Council and the dispute between Paul and Peter that I described in chapter 4 did not lay the argument about the Law in general and circumcision in particular to rest; indeed the way Paul's thought developed on the question remains a central theme running through almost all his writing. In the last chapter I reflected on the way he used the language of his letters to create a sense of a family of faith, a community that transcended traditional ties of city and kinship. The flip side of that is the language of extreme violence he directs toward his enemies; no one can deliver a verbal mugging quite like Paul. The targets of his most vicious sallies tend to be Jews, and especially Jews who believe, like him, in the teachings of Jesus, but disagree with him on this central issue. I have quoted his unexpected explosion in the Letter to the Philippians earlier: "Beware of the dogs, beware of the evil workers, beware of those who mutilate the flesh!" (Phil 3:2). To the Galatians ("You foolish Galatians! Who has bewitched you? Gal 3:1) he writes of "false believers secretly brought in, who slipped in to spy on the freedom we have in Christ Jesus, so that they might enslave us" (Gal 2:4), and later in the letter, in what it is all too easy to see as a passing jibe at the practice of circumcision, he declares, "I wish those who unsettle you would castrate themselves!" (Gal 5:12).

"Once you've been circumcised," the mohel Dr. Cooper pointed out, "you can't really drop out. You may not observe all the commandments, but you are a Jew and you can never lose that." Circumcision is every bit as central to Jewish identity as it is to the theology of Judaism, and that is why the debate provoked by Paul's stand slips beyond the bounds of theology, into very raw territory indeed. In this chapter I shall assess his role in the long and shameful history of anti-Semitism. It would, of course, be grotesque to "blame" Paul for the Holocaust, or the pogroms that took place in Russia nineteen centuries after his death. Our view of him is bound to be colored by our own awareness of what has been done in the name of Christian and European anti-Semitism in times much closer to our own than to his, and we need to be acutely aware of that when we judge him. But it is an inescapable fact that the argument between Jews and Christians really begins with Paul, and the tortured relationship between Judaism and Christianity has been an extraordinarily powerful force in our history. Paul's divisive legacy has proved depressingly enduring. His ideal of Christian fellowship gave birth to the concepts of Christendom and a united universal Christian church; both are long gone. But the divisions between Jew and Christian that he left behind are still very much with us, and the grave charge that he is the father of anti-Semitism has to be addressed.

Most of the hard evidence we have about Paul's views on his fellow Jews comes from the letters written on his third missionary journey, which is usually dated in the early 50s. His time in Jerusalem and Antioch on his return from Corinth seems to have been reasonably brief—before long those eager feet took him back through Asia Minor, checking up on the churches he had founded like an anxious fisherman inspecting his lobster pots. A new chapter opens with his arrival at the great city of Ephesus, another of those hubs so well suited to the dissemination of his message across the empire. Paul settled here for at least two years, and this third missionary journey covers the period when we can come closest to his mind. The dating of his letters is a scholarly hornet's nest, but it seems likely he wrote several of them during his time in Ephesus, and most of the rest during his visit to Greece on the second leg of the same journey.

The situation Paul found when he arrived in Ephesus gives an insight into the very fluid and dynamic state of Christianity some two decades after the crucifixion. Paul had been to Ephesus before—he dropped in on his way back from Corinth at the end of the second missionary journey—but since his visit the city had been evangelized by one Apollos, a Jew from Alexandria who seems to have had a slightly uncertain grasp on what Paul regarded as orthodoxy. So when Paul arrives he finds "some disciples" who, when questioned about their beliefs, definitely fail the catechism: "He said to them, 'Did you receive the Holy Spirit when you became believers?' They replied, 'No, we have not even heard that there is a Holy Spirit.' Then he said, 'Into what then were you baptized?' They replied, 'Into John's baptism'" (Acts 19:2–3). Paul of course puts them right and has them rebaptized. One forms the impression of a thoroughly confusing religious marketplace, with several different versions of Christianity on offer. The church was very much a work in progress at this stage, and Paul seems to have spent a good deal of his time swatting eruptions of heresy. The idea that circumcision and the Law were necessary to salvation was by far the most persistent.

It is in that context that Paul developed what scholars are pleased to call his "antinomianism." Jesus, according to some studies of the New Testament, was what might be called "Torah neutral." "Do not," he tells the crowds gathered to hear the Sermon on the Mount, "think that I have come to abolish the law or the prophets; I have come not to abolish but fulfill. For truly I tell you, until heaven and earth pass away, not one letter, not one stroke of a letter, will pass away from the law until all is accomplished" (Matt 5:17-18). There are moments when Paul's position seems to be similar; in his account of the Jerusalem Council, for example, he suggests some kind of equality between Jewish believers in Jesus who continue to observe the Law and Gentile believers who do not: "I had been entrusted with the gospel for the uncircumcised, just as Peter had been entrusted with the gospel for the circumcised" (Gal 2:7). And the Acts of the Apostles account of the compromise reached at the same meeting suggests that at this stage Paul was willing to show some deference to the idea of Law for form's sake; the council asked Gentile Christians "to abstain only from things polluted by idols and from fornication and from whatever has been strangled and from blood" (Acts 15:20). But Paul soon moved on to the more aggressive position known as antinomianism: he did not simply argue that the Law was a neutral irrelevance that had been superseded by Christ; he often seems to present it as something that was actively malign.

The classic statement of Paul's antinomianism comes in a passage in the Letter to the Galatians, which, for reasons I shall explore later, became a central text of the Reformation several centuries afterwards: "Stand firm, therefore, and do not submit again to a yoke of slavery. Listen! I, Paul, am telling you that if you let yourselves be circumcised, Christ will be of no benefit to you.... You who want to be justified by the law have cut yourselves off from Christ; you have fallen away from grace" (Gal 5:1-2, 4). It is difficult to imagine anything more insulting to Jews than the description of their Torah as a "yoke of slavery," and the message to Christian converts here is unambiguous; follow the Law and you might as well stop calling yourselves Christians, because Christianity and the Law are mutually exclusive.

Jerome Murphy O'Connor offers a plausible explanation for Paul adopting such a hard-line position at this point. It depends on us accepting the case for a relatively late dating of the Letter to the Galatians, but I find it convincing. A group of "Judaizers," Father Murphy O'Connor argues, moved into Galatia after Paul's departure for Ephesus and set about persuading the converts in the churches there that the Law was essential to salvation. As part of their campaign they sought to discredit Paul, whom they accused of proclaiming a half-baked version of Jesus' message. Father Murphy O'Connor quotes a notional speech these Judaizers might have addressed to Paul's wavering disciples:

> You say you have been converted by Paul? We say that you are still in a darkness entirely similar to the darkness in which not long ago you were serving the elements, supposing them, as Abraham once did, to be gods that rule the world. In fact the fights and contentions in your communities show that you have not really been converted, that Paul did not give you God's holy guidance. Paul left you, a group of sailors on the treacherous high seas, in nothing more than a small and poorly equipped boat.

By contrast they brought a Law that offered security and certainty (of the kind, indeed, that certain forms of evangelical Christianity offer today). It is easy to see how Paul would have taken the challenge to his authority very personally when word of what was happening in the Galatian churches reached him in Ephesus (or Corinth, if you belong to the school that dates the Letter to the Galatians even later). He was extremely thin-skinned on the issue of his claim to a place among the first rank of the apostles. He had never known Jesus during his life, and his letters are full of remarks that show how vulnerable that made him feel; indeed the biographical résumé with which Paul opens the Letter to the Galatians is clearly an attempt to defend his apostolic authority. Furthermore the news that some of his very earliest converts had been so easily seduced could quite reasonably have led him to the conclusion that the Law was a powerful and dangerous force that needed to be taken on and fought wherever it showed itself.

However, the fact that there is a convincing explanation for Paul flying off the handle when he wrote to the Galatians does not alter the fact that for many Jews it is extremely offensive. The Letter to the Galatians is Exhibit A in the case against Paul on charges of responsibility for Christian anti-Semitism.

Defense counsel might reasonably point out that Paul was himself Jewish, and that anti-Semitism of a kind had been around for some time in the ancient world. The story of Moses' flight from Egypt in Exodus, after all, begins with an eerily modern-sounding attempt at genocide by a national leader who fears the Jews are taking over his country: "Now a new king arose over Egypt, who did not know Joseph. He said to his people, 'Look, the Israelite people are more numerous and more powerful than we" (Exod 1:8–9). His solution was to instruct midwives that they should kill all male Jewish children. According to Dan Cohn-Sherbok in his study *Anti-Semitism: A History,* the Jews suffered from the general Hellenistic view that "anything non-Greek was uncivilised." Roman attitudes toward the Jews are suggested by a diatribe in a speech by Cicero in 59 BC, when the great orator was defending his political ally Flaccus against charges of "rapine and oppression" during his time as governor of Asia. Each year the Jews of the Diaspora would collect gold from around the Roman world and send it to Jerusalem, and Flaccus had been condemned for stopping this custom, taking the gold and sending it to Rome. Cicero argues that he should be praised, not blamed for this, because "to despise the multitude of Jews…was an act of the greatest wisdom." The Jews, he says, are "odious," and "the religious ceremonies and observances of that people were very much at variance with the splendor of this empire." The Roman suppression of the Jewish revolt in AD 70 was unusually brutal even by Roman standards, and the destruction of the Temple was self-evidently designed as a fatal blow to the Jewish sense of identity and nationhood (although the Romans would no doubt have explained it away as a necessary security measure rather than the expression of anything as abstract as anti-Semitism). But Christian anti-Semitism is different in kind: more passionate, somehow

103

more personal, and certainly more enduring. And Paul is the first Christian writer.

It is salutary to read your own history through the eyes of others. This is Dan Cohn-Sherbok's summary of the New Testament:

> Christian animosity (towards the Jews) was fuelled by the Gospel writers, who depicted Jesus attacking the leaders of the nation.... In proclaiming the good news, Paul emphasised that the Hebrew people had been rejected by God; Christ is the true eternal Temple in opposition to the earthly cult of Jerusalem. Such a contrast is to be found in the Fourth Gospel, which differentiates between the spiritual universe of Christianity and a fallen world represented by Jews.

This seems to be rather harsh on Paul; he does not say that God has rejected the Jews, he says that the Jews have rejected God. But Dan Cohn-Sherbok draws an even more damning picture of Paul's attitude from the Letter to the Galatians: "For Paul," he writes, "the Torah is synonymous with the domination of demonic powers." It is certainly true that Paul presents the Law as a rather unsatisfactory way of dealing with sin while the world awaited the Messiah: "It [the law] was added because of transgressions.... Now before faith came, we were imprisoned and guarded under the law" (Gal 3:19, 23). Cohn-Sherbok concludes his study of the letter with the following judgment on Paul's theology:

> The Church has not simply superseded Judaism. Rather, the two faiths are opposed to each other. Judaism belongs to the realm of fallen Adam, but Christianity fulfils the divine promises recorded in Scripture. Those who belong to the Moses covenant will be cast out, but the children of the new covenant will be saved in Christ. Paul's diatribe against the Jews is thus a rejection of the Jewish tradition.

Paul the Divider

The most sustained recent attack on Paul from a Talmudic scholar is Hyam Maccoby's *The Mythmaker: Paul and the Invention of Christianity*. The book's "warfare on the time-honoured beliefs about the origins of Christianity" is conducted on all fronts; Jesus features as a Pharisee who had "no intention of founding a new religion. He regarded himself as the Messiah in the normal Jewish sense of the term, i.e. a human leader who would restore the Jewish monarchy, drive out the Roman invaders, set up an independent Jewish state, and inaugurate an era of peace, justice and prosperity (known as the 'kingdom of god') for the whole world," while Paul, by contrast, claimed to be a Pharisee but was not one, and emerges as a brilliant, tortured, highly imaginative and unscrupulous religious opportunist. Jesus, Maccoby argues, would have regarded the religion Paul created in his name "with consternation."

This is not the place for a comprehensive assessment of Hyam Maccoby's theories, but his conclusions bear directly on the issue of Paul's alleged anti-Semitism. "It was Paul," he declares, "who detached Jesus from his mission of liberation and turned him into an otherworldly figure whose mission had no relevance to politics or to the suffering of his fellow Jews under the Romans. This transformation had the effect of making the Jews, instead of the Romans, responsible for Jesus' crucifixion." Maccoby claims that Paul was heavily influenced by the shadowy belief system known as Gnosticism (I have read several accounts of it and still do not understand what it means; I am not completely convinced that anyone else does). Paul, he says, "sharpened and intensified the anti-Semitism already present in Gnosticism." Since Paul argued that faith in Jesus had superseded the Law, there was "an incentive to blacken the Jewish record in order to justify the Christian take-over of the Abrahamic 'promises.'"

And because Paul's letters predate the four gospels, he is held responsible for the way they treat the Jewish people: "The myth adumbrated by Paul was then brought to full imaginative life in the Gospels, which were written under the influence of Paul's ideas and for the use of the Pauline Church." The figure of Judas, the quintessential betrayer, is held up as a particularly vicious Jewish stereotype, and Maccoby cites the way the crowds

105

call for Christ's crucifixion and Barabbas's freedom as another example of the way the gospels demonize the Jews: "What in Paul's letters was only the outline of a myth has become definite and replete with narrative quality, an instrument for cultural indoctrination and the conveyor of indelible impressions to children who are told the tale."

I do not recognize Hyam Maccoby's Paul. I find it difficult to accept, for example, that he would have blown a good part of the money he had collected for the poor of Jerusalem to buy himself Roman citizenship, as Maccoby alleges without, it seems to me, very much evidence; that sort of deviousness does not match the character of the Paul I meet in the letters. But I am of course approaching the apostle with the intellectual baggage of a Christian education and upbringing. I have been struck again and again during the reading I have done for this book by the way even the most rigorous scholars allow their view of the historical Paul to be colored by their own inclinations, by the attitudes of their age, and sometimes by prejudice. Paul is a central figure in the faith that first allowed me to make some kind of sense of the world, so I am naturally disposed to give him the benefit of the many doubts that arise about his life and writing.

When I discussed Paul in Jerusalem, however, I was meeting people who came to him from a very different religious perspective, and it brought home to me even more forcefully how difficult it is for Jews and Christians—or even cultural Christians and secular Jews—to escape Paul's intellectual legacy. Ideas that were revolutionary when he articulated them are today's natural assumptions—or at least they have always seemed so to me. But I discovered that that is, of course, certainly not true for everyone. I have several times quoted the passage in the Letter to the Galatians where Paul declares that the old divisions by race, gender, or social status have been superseded by unity in Christ; it seems to me an inspiring expression of an idea that is self-evidently a Good Thing, and even if you take Christ out of the equation Paul's vision of human fellowship is surely something to be admired. But Rabbi David Rosen—who is in charge of relations between different faiths for the American Jewish Committee in Jerusalem—identified this idea as the very heart of the problem.

The sense of Jewish identity rests on the idea that Jews are different, with a special mission for humanity, and the Law is a mark of that difference. Paul, he said, "pulled away the structure of definition of Jewish identity": "The moment you say we are no different from other families...and that the criteria by which we define the community by law are no longer pertinent, then you've basically undermined the very ethos of the Jewish community." The rabbi was an engaging and highly intelligent man, eager to explore Christian ideas (that, after all, is part of his job), and I hope I came to our discussion with an open mind about Judaism; yet there we were, trapped on different sides of an intellectual ditch that Paul dug two thousand years ago.

Yossi Klein Halevi, the religious affairs correspondent of the news magazine *Jerusalem Report,* was with us in the agreeable offices of the American Jewish Committee, and he argued that Paul's real crime was the way he allowed the outside world to eavesdrop on what should have remained a quarrel within the Jewish family. The very sharp tone of Paul's debating techniques is, he observed, all too familiar in debates about the Talmud between rabbis, but it can become anti-Semitic if it is used by outsiders. Both he and David Rosen saw an analogy between the impact of Paul's writing and the way Israel is treated by the foreign press today. "So much of the Israeli anger towards much of the world media and the way Israel is judged," Yossi Klein Halevi said, "relates precisely to this point about the way outsiders will eavesdrop on our own, internal debate, extract the criticism by Israelis, and present that as a judgment against Israel, against the State of Israel." Rabbi Rosen revealed that when he is campaigning on human rights issues in Israel he deliberately moderates the tone of his criticism of the government if he is talking to the outside world—unlike Paul, who lets rip with the kind of colorful invective that is a headline-writer's dream.

To trace Paul's influence on Christian anti-Semitism over the past two thousand years would be a vast scholarly undertaking well beyond the scope of this book, but it is worth reflecting on the way his name has an eerie habit of cropping up in association with moments of heresy, division, and schism in religious history. The first serious heresy the church faced, Marcionism, was based

on the conviction that Paul was the only apostle who really understood Christ's significance. Marcion, the son of the bishop of
Sinope (all sorts of things worked differently in the Catholic
Church of those days), argued that there were two Gods, a
Supreme God of goodness and an inferior God of Justice, who
was the God of the Jews. He regarded Christ as the messenger of
the Supreme God.

Marcion established a canon of sacred writing to reflect
those views; it included ten Pauline letters (Galatians, 1 and 2
Corinthians, Romans, 1 and 2 Thessalonians, Ephesians,
Colossians, Philemon, and Philippians) and Luke's Gospel, but
excluded the whole of the Old Testament and all the other
gospels of the New Testament (Luke's presumably survived
because of his association with Paul). Even those texts that
Marcion regarded as genuine did not entirely escape his ideological scalpel; any passage that he considered a Judaizing corruption
of Christian purity was simply removed. So even though he
regarded Paul's Letter to the Galatians as the most important
Christian text of all, he excised Paul's reflections on the children
of Abraham in chapter 4, on the grounds that they suggested an
inappropriate connection between Christianity and Judaism. This
astonishingly ambitious attempt to cut Christianity free from any
association with its roots in Judaism was condemned by the
church in Rome in AD 144, but the heresy was not completely
defeated in the Eastern Church until the tenth century.

Martin Luther, like Marcion, saw the Letter to the Galatians as
the key to the treasure-house of Christian truth, and his massive,
verse-by-verse commentary on Galatians is one of the central books
of the Reformation. Luther took what Paul wrote about the Jews
and applied it to the Catholic Church, so what in Paul was the
source of the split between Judaism and Christianity becomes in
Luther the rationale for the division between Catholicism and
Protestantism. The pivotal passage in Galatians that I quoted earlier
in this chapter—"I, Paul, am telling you that if you let yourselves be
circumcised, Christ will be of no benefit to you"—is for Luther "a
touchstone, whereby we may freely judge of all doctrines, works,
religions, and ceremonies of men." "Whosoever teaches," he thun-
ders on, "that there is anything necessary to salvation (whether they

be Papists, Turks, Jews, or sectaries) besides faith in Christ, or shall devise any work or religion, or observe any rule, tradition, or ceremony whatsoever, with this opinion, that by such things they shall obtain forgiveness of sins, righteousness, and everlasting life; they hear in this place the sentence of the Holy Ghost pronounced against them by the apostle, that Christ profiteth them nothing." Luther clearly admires Paul's vigorous use of language (he paints, with obvious delight, a picture of the apostle "wonderfully stirred up with zeal and fervency of spirit," who "thundereth against the law and circumcision") and he sets about his enemies with a Pauline relish ("Wherefore this place," he writes of the passage quoted above, "is a terrible thunderbolt against all the kingdom of the Pope").

Whether Luther's admiration for Paul played a part in his anti-Semitism is obviously difficult to judge. When Luther's original hopes that Jews would be attracted to his purified brand of Christianity were rebuffed he turned violently against them. His book *The Jews and Their Lies* is one of the most disgusting texts in Christian history, recommending, among other things, the burning of synagogues and Jewish schools, the razing of Jewish homes (the Jews should, he says, live in communal barns), the suppression of rabbinical teaching, and the mass deportation of Jews from Germany. And Luther picked up with enthusiasm on the stereotypes Hyam Maccoby complains about in the New Testament. In another attack on the Jews, Luther wrote:

> Cursed goy that I am, I cannot understand how they manage to be so skillful, unless I think that when Judas Iscariot hanged himself, his guts burst open and emptied. Perhaps the Jews sent their servants with plates of silver and pots of gold to gather up Judas' piss with the other treasures, and they ate his offal, and thereby acquired eyes so piercing that they discover in the Scriptures commentaries that neither Matthew nor Isaiah himself found there, not to mention the rest of us cursed goyim.

But if we are going to condemn Paul for some of his admirers we should also praise him for some of his enemies. It is one of the great paradoxes of the Pauline legacy that a figure so much associated with Christian anti-Semitism should also be hated by perhaps the greatest anti-Semite of them all: Adolf Hitler. Hitler is a prominent name on the long list of those who believe that Paul distorted the purity of the original Jesus message, although his particular angle on this idea is rather more eccentric than most. "It is certain," he told his inner circle of admirers one lunchtime in October 1941, "that Jesus was not a Jew"; Hitler rather bizarrely suggests that he was the son of a Roman legionnaire who became "a popular leader who took up his position against Jewry." Paul, by contrast, Hitler saw as very much a Jew with a Jewish agenda, someone who exploited Jesus' authority and corrupted his teaching for his own purposes: "The decisive falsification of Jesus' doctrine was the work of St. Paul," Hitler declares. "When he learned that Jesus' supporters let their throats be cut for his ideas, he realized that, by making intelligent use of the Galilean's teaching, it would be possible to overthrow this Roman state that the Jews hated." According to this version of history, Paul's successful evangelization becomes a means for spreading a wicked Jewish conspiracy throughout Europe under the guise of a new religion, and in another of the conversations recorded in *Table Talk* Hitler declares that the coming of Christianity was the "heaviest blow that had ever struck humanity." That remark was made on the night of July 11, 1941, just after Hitler's invasion of the Soviet Union: "Bolshevism is Christianity's illegitimate child. Both are inventions of the Jew," he added for good measure. So Paul is really responsible for pretty much everything that Hitler believed was wrong with twentieth-century Europe. He called Paul the "first man to take advantage of using religion as a means of propaganda," and labeled his beliefs "crypto-Marxist"—which was at the very least somewhat anachronistic.

Hitler's rantings about Paul were a distorted echo of those of Nietzsche, yet another German who was obsessed by the apostle. The rejection of what Nietzsche called the "slave morality" of the Judaeo-Christian tradition was central to his philosophy. Nietzsche believed that in the natural order of things power and holiness were one and the same, and he argued that the Jews, driven by the rancor the weak feel against the strong (*ressentiment* he called it) had turned that moral system on its head with their ethical monotheism. It was, he wrote, "the Jews who with awe-inspiring consistency dared to invert the aristocratic value equation (good=noble=powerful=beautiful=happy=beloved of God) and to hang on to this 'inversion' with all their strength." Christianity accordingly becomes the means by which this slave morality is introduced into the Gentile world, fatally undermining the aristocratic value system of the Roman Empire, and subsequently infecting all of Europe with its decadence. And Paul is the evil genius who brings about this epoch-changing act of Jewish vengeance. For Nietzsche, Paul is not Christ's evangelist but his enemy:

> In Paul was embodied the antithetical type to the "bringer of glad tidings"; the genius of hatred, of the vision of hatred, of the inexorable logic of hatred. *What* did this dysangelist not sacrifice to his hatred! The redeemer above all; he nailed him to *his* cross. The life, the example, the teaching, the death, the meaning, and the right of the entire gospel—nothing was left once this hate-obsessed false-coiner had grasped what alone he could make use of.

Like Hitler, Nietzsche accuses Paul of developing doctrines that were never in Christ's mind, the resurrection among them: "Paul, with that rabbinical insolence that characterizes him in every respect, rationalizes this interpretation, this *indecency* of an interpretation, thus 'If Christ is not resurrected from the dead our faith is in vain.'" And through Paul the Jewish spirit takes over Europe in a new guise: "The Christian," declares Nietzsche, "is only a Jew of a 'freer' confession."

With that we come a dizzying full circle. On the one hand, Paul is accused of corrupting the essentially Jewish message of Jesus and turning it into an alien faith that spawned anti-Semitism—on the other, he is accused of subverting Christ's teaching for precisely the opposite purpose, so that he can exert his baleful Jewish influence over whole of Western civilization. During the writing of this book I was making frequent trips to the United States, and with all those hours of dead time in the air above the Atlantic I frequently fell prey to the temptations of the bookshops at Dulles and JFK airports. On one trip I picked up a new American novel by Joseph Skibell called *The English Disease*, which in this context meant neither industrial unrest nor football hooliganism, but melancholia. The hero is a Jewish American musicologist who becomes obsessed by the conviction that he has done violence to his roots by marrying a beautiful blond Gentile. At one point he decides that divorce is the only option—even though his marriage is a happy one—and tries to explain his decision to his wife Isabelle:

> ...it had less to do with me, quite frankly, than with Paul of Tarsus, whose first century break with the other Jewish followers of Jesus over the issue of missionizing the Gentiles had been decisive and schismatic.
>
> 'Oh Charles, please don't bring up Paul of Tarsus now' Isabelle says.

But people do keep bringing him up—endlessly. And somehow his name always seems to be associated with arguments.

If you approach the Ummayad Mosque in Damascus through the Hamidiye Souk, you pass under the Roman gateway, or *propylaeum,* of what was once the temple of Jupiter. Its austere columns rise from amid the market stalls, and a broken pediment floats serenely and somewhat incongruously above all this colorful and chaotic commerce. The site has been sacred for at least three millennia, but no one has quite matched the Romans in architectural ambition; the temple compound was vast, stretching well over 330 yards eastward from the gate, and in the lower parts of the mosque walls you can still see the huge Roman blocks of stone that were reused by a later generation.

At the mosque ticket office I was handed a pamphlet that celebrated the glorious achievement of President Hafez al-Assad in restoring the buildings to their former glory, but told me very little about their extraordinary history. The Ummayad Mosque is in fact a religious palimpsest; it was successively a Roman temple (when St. Paul visited the city), a Christian basilica, and one of the greatest monuments of early Islam, and each belief system has left its architectural mark. Most of what you see today was built in the early eighth century, some seventy years after the Muslim conquest of Damascus. But the prayer hall was constructed on the site of the old basilica, and with its transepts and aisles it looks very much like an early Christian church; I found my eyes constantly led downward toward the eastern wall where all my instincts told me to expect a sanctuary and an altar.

The mosque complex contains two highly suggestive symbols of the history of the relationship between Christianity and Islam—one a reminder of ancient hostilities, the other a monument to intimate connections. Just outside the north wall of the main courtyard is the tomb of Saladin, the brilliant twelfth-century military leader who managed to unite the Muslim world against the Crusaders and drive them out of Jerusalem; it is a relatively unassuming structure and was, by one of those odd quirks of history, given a makeover by Kaiser Wilhelm II in 1898 as part of his Ottoman charm offensive. Much more striking is the green, gold, and marble shrine that sits inside the prayer hall itself—it is the size of modest chapel, and has a dome all of its own, and its presence inside the building serves to emphasize the epic scale of the place. The story goes that when the mosque was being built men working in the crypt found a crate with a copper box inside; the caliph himself was called on site to inspect, and the box was found to carry an inscription declaring that it contained the head of John the Baptist. The caliph decreed that it should be left in its place, and the shrine now marks the spot.

John, or Yahya as he is known in Islam, is venerated by Muslims as well as Christians. He is one of the twenty-five prophets mentioned in the Koran, and I watched people shove scribbled prayers and money into the grillwork that protects the arched green windows surrounding his head's final resting place. I had a professional guide with me, Malik Kashcara, and he said that most people in the city, Muslims as well as Christians, take pride in its place in Christian history—he pointed out that Damascus had Christianity a good half a millennium before it reached England. But when I asked about people's attitude to Paul the picture became more cloudy; of course, Malik answered, there is a certain civic pride taken in the fact that Damascus has such a strong association with a towering figure of history. But Paul's theology, he explained, makes him an extremely troubling figure for Muslims. I found myself opening another—entirely unexpected—chapter in the history of Paul the divider.

Many aspects of the Islamic Jesus would be familiar to Christians. The Koran gives him a virgin birth, and records the annunciation—when an angel tells Mary that she will bear a son—in terms very similar to those of the New Testament. Muslim tradition includes the story of the three Wise Men following their star with gold, frankincense, and myrrh, and a version of the New Testament account of Jesus turning the water into wine at a marriage feast. Jesus, like John the Baptist, is regarded as one of the twenty-five prophets by Muslims, and the Koran accords him a special dignity, declaring him to be "eminent in this world and the next, one of those who approach God's presence." But what Muhammad could simply not accept was the idea of a divine Christ.

Muhammad insisted that he was not proclaiming a new religion, merely restating the one true religion that had been given to humanity since the beginning, and he believed that all the prophets that preceded him had brought essentially the same message. God kept sending new prophets with new revelations because of humanity's tendency to fall away from the truth, and Jesus was simply part of that process. The Koran puts it like this: "Jesus, son of Mary, said, 'O Children of Israel, truly I am God's messenger to you verifying what was before me with respect to the Torah and bringing good news of an apostle who will come after me whose name will be Ahmad.'" In that context the idea that Jesus was the son of God and was himself divine represented a terrible heresy, and the Christian concept of the Trinity was an almost pagan departure from Muhammad's uncompromising monotheism. Thus this passage in the Koran:

> O people of the Book, do not be fanatical in your religion, and do not say anything but the truth about God. The Messiah, Jesus son of Mary, is only God's apostle and his Word which He cast into Mary, and a spirit from him. So believe in God and his apostles, and do

114

not say, 'He is three.' Eschew, and it will be better for you. God is only one God. Far be it from him that he should have a son!

In another Koranic reflection on the nature of Jesus it is put even more simply: "They have disbelieved who said, 'Indeed God is the third of three,' when there is no God but one God."

Moreover, Muslim tradition questions those central tenets of the Christian faith, Jesus' crucifixion and resurrection; the early Islamic writer Wahb bin Munnabih suggested that Jesus was taken up into heaven by God while a "simulacrum" was crucified in his place, and the tenth-century Koranic scholar Al-Tha'labi took the idea a stage further by proposing that Judas was nailed to the cross in Jesus' place; when Jesus was brought to the cross, he wrote, "darkness covered the earth, and God sent angels who took up their position between Jesus and the executioners. The countenance of Jesus was placed on Judas, who had betrayed him, and [they] crucified him instead, supposing that he was Jesus. After three hours God took Jesus to himself and raised him up to the kingdom of heaven."

The elements of Christian theology and tradition that are most offensive to Islam are, of course, precisely those that lie at the heart of Paul's teaching. The divinity of Christ is the foundation for his entire mission; his own account of his conversion is summed up in that very simple sentence "God...was pleased to reveal his Son to me" (Gal 1:15). His whole approach to religion assumes that the history of humanity's relationship with God is dynamic, an unfolding process that culminates in Christ. He would obviously have been outraged at the idea that Jesus was "verifying what was before me with respect to the Torah," because, as we have seen, he spent most of his life trying to persuade people that Jesus had made the Law redundant. And the reality of Jesus' death and resurrection was for him the key to salvation. He states quite explicitly (in one of the passages quoted above that gave such offense to Nietzsche), that unless Christ died and rose again nothing makes any sense, and if he had not believed that, he could never have forged Christ's death and resurrection into the uniquely powerful religious metaphor it became in his hands. In the Letter to the Philippians there is a famous hymn to Jesus; it is now thought that Paul was probably quoting a piece of poetry written by someone else (perhaps one of his own converts) at this point, but it is as good an expression as there is of who he thought Jesus was. "Let the same mind be in you," he writes, "that was in Christ Jesus,

> who, though he was in the form of God,
>   did not regard equality with God
>   as something to be exploited,
> but emptied himself,
>   taking the form of a slave,
>   being born in human likeness.
> And being found in human form,
>   he humbled himself
>   and became obedient to the point of death—
>   even death on a cross.
>
> Therefore God also highly exalted him
>   and gave him the name
>   that is above every name,
> so that at the name of Jesus
>   every knee should bend,
>   in heaven and on earth and under the earth,
> and every tongue should confess
>   that Jesus Christ is Lord
>   to the glory of God the Father. (Phil 2:5–11)

And so it is that Paul, condemned as the father of anti-Semitism and hated by Hitler, becomes Islam's chief villain too. Ibn Taymiyyah, a twelfth-century Islamic scholar and controversialist from Damascus (his father preached in the Umayyad Mosque), accuses him of fabrication "when he entered into the religion of Christianity in order to corrupt the religion of the Christians." More recently there have been Islamic attacks on Paul from a position very close to that of Hyam Maccoby: "Surely in this present age," the contemporary British Muslim writer Ruqaiyyah Waris Maqsood suggests, "when scholarly literature about the religious atmosphere of the time is readily available, has the moment not come to consider seriously the painful but inescapable question of whether Paul's theology was what Jesus actually taught?" She continues, "Without the tragedy of Paul's sudden insight into 'mystery religion' theology, the Mother-Church might have reformed Judaism into a new spirituality," and established itself as the "true, universal world-faith." A trawl of the Internet, where people seem to feel comfortable expressing anger and prejudice in polemics, produced some pretty nasty stuff; one essay I found called Paul the "corrupter" of Christianity, another claimed that he was a "clear-cut hypocrite" and a "snake." And an equally militant Christian Web site I turned up described Paul as "the man who Muslims love to hate."

7

Paul the Moralist

The state of the Corinthian Church resembles, in a remarkable degree, the state of the Church of this Town in the present day. There is the same complicated civilisation, the same questions agitate society, and the same distinctions of class exist now as then. For the heart of Humanity is the same in all times. The principles, therefore, which St Paul applied to the Corinthian questions will apply to those of this time.

What on earth was going on in Brighton, England, in 1851, when the Reverend F. W. Robertson delivered the first of his "Lectures on Corinthians" to his congregation at the town's Trinity Chapel? Incest? Sacred prostitution? Ritual slaughter? Was idol worship a big problem? Or speaking in tongues? Were his parishioners turning up at church drunk on a regular basis? Brighton had a certain louche reputation at the beginning of the 1800s, but if would be surprising if in the high Victorian era it was awash with fornication and sodomy. The issue of veils for women was no doubt sometimes debated, but presumably for reasons of fashion rather then piety. If the Reverend Robertson's Brighton really was "agitated" by the questions that preoccupied first-century Corinth, then it must have been a very odd place indeed.

The Corinth of Paul's time was in fact about as atypical as it was possible to be; its culture was extremely distinctive then, and certainly very different from ours today. Even the briefest and most superficial reading of his correspondence with the Corinthians is enough to bring home that he was writing to a particular community at a particular time, and that his advice is designed for a very particular set of problems. But the two letters to the Corinthians that have become part of the biblical canon lie at the heart of the debate about how all his letters should be read. Are they simply intriguing documents of social history that tell us about the preoccupations of first-century society, or should today's Christians regard them as the voice of God speaking through Paul, laying down rules that should be applied by all men and women in all times, as the Reverend Robertson clearly believed?

There is an unmistakably universal and timeless tone about the way Paul hands down some of his instructions in his correspondence with Corinth, and his rulings on such topics as marriage, divorce, homosexuality, and the role of women have provided the foundations for much of Christian ethics. The Corinthian letters are the mine from which a Pauline moral system has been quarried by later generations of priests and prelates and—especially—Protestant theologians. The Paul they have hewn out of history for us in the process is the familiar Paul of my conventional Christian upbringing—thundering away and forbidding things in language that often seemed to come from a remote time and place. Here he is in full flow: "Do you not know that wrongdoers will not inherit the kingdom of God? Do not be deceived! Fornicators, idolaters, adulterers, male prostitutes, sodomites, thieves, the greedy, drunkards, revilers, robbers—none of these will inherit the kingdom of God" (1 Cor 6:9–10).

Corinth had a reputation for loose morals that was originally associated with the practice of sacred prostitution. Aphrodite, the Greek goddess of love, was the city's protector, and her temple was at the heart of Corinth's acropolis—sitting 1,800 feet above sea level on a stark and impregnable lump of rock with magnificent views across the isthmus toward mainland Greece. Strabo, the geographer and travel writer born in the mid-60s BC, records that "the temple of Aphrodite was so rich that it owned more than a thousand temple slaves, courtesans whom both men and women had dedicated to the goddess. And therefore it was also on account of these women that the city was crowded with people and grew rich." Quite how the practice of sacred prostitution worked no one really seems to know. Herodotus records a Babylonian version of the custom that decreed that "every woman who is a native of the country must once in her life go and sit in the temple of Aphrodite and there give herself to a strange man." He says the women would sit in roped-off areas waiting for strangers to make a choice by throwing a coin—rather as one might to a street performer today—and states that "those of the women as are tall and beautiful are soon released," while those less well favored sometimes waited "two or three years" before getting through this dubious hurdle to full adulthood. In Corinth the prostitutes may simply have been a source of temple income, and the custom may anyway have belonged to a period that long predates Paul's involvement with the city. Corinth was razed to the ground in 146 BC for an act of revolt against Rome—the Romans especially objected to the way its rebellious citizens threw turds into their chariots as they passed—and for a century it was home only to a few squatters who lived among the ruins; when it was refounded as a Roman colony by Julius Caesar in 44 BC it was populated largely by freed slaves from around the empire to whom the custom of sacred prostitution would have been quite alien.

Nevertheless the city's association with the kind of lewd carryings-on that provides the backdrop to Paul's correspondence with the city's Christians continued in the use of the Greek word *korinthiazomai* to mean fornicate, and the extraordinary speed with which the reborn Corinth revived its fortunes contributed to a racy lifestyle. Corinth's unique selling point was its capacity to provide a bridge between the Aegean and the Ionian seas; merchants and shipowners could avoid the 600-mile journey around the Peloponnese by the simple expedient of unloading at one of Corinth's two harbors (Lechaeum and Cenchreae), and carrying their goods (and sometimes even their ships too) four miles across land to the other. By the time of Paul's visit Corinth had expanded to cover an area bigger than that of ancient Athens, and it was the most populous city in Greece. H. V. Morton pictures

> a city built on a narrow neck of land, with the eastern harbour full of Egyptian, Asiatic and Phoenician galleys, while the western harbour was full of the cargo-boats of Italy, Spain, and the Adriatic. Wagons must have been constantly crossing the few miles from

120

Cenchreae with the goods of Egypt, Asia Minor and Syria for transhipment to the west at Lechaeum; and a reverse line of wagons from Lechaeum must have carried western merchandise to Cenchreae for transhipment to the Orient. No wonder that Corinth, situated between two such ports, developed a cosmopolitanism tinged with the vices of the foreign nations whose ships lay in her harbours.

There is certainly archaeological evidence that the trade and the money brought a demand for entertainment in their wake. Dr. Guy Sanders is in charge of excavations in Corinth—he works for the American School of Classical Studies in Athens but is very much the stylish British amateur in manner, and he strode around the site followed by the sort of dog that would look more at home on a grouse moor, showing off his patch rather as if it were his private estate. In a narrow alley just behind the city's theater (East Theater Street, he calls it), he has turned up ovens and burnt bones that he says indicate the existence of "a couple of fast-food joints," and he has found a hint that this may have been Corinth's red-light district in a complex that he has excavated just across the way; it was decorated with frescoes of Aphrodite admiring her beauty in the mirror of her shield, and he found a number of erotic terracotta figures in one of the rooms. Dr. Sanders recalled studying as an undergraduate at Southampton University:

> I lived on a street which was infamous for the number of prostitutes that worked there, and I remember on one occasion when a large American air force carrier docked at Southampton, and for about three days afterwards there were long queues of American sailors— thirty or forty men long—standing outside the houses. In many respects I imagine that is what Corinth was like in certain quarters when a new ship came in.

Roman Corinth was little more than a century old when Paul made his first visit there, and because it was so young and rich it was also an extremely dynamic society, with plenty of brash new money around and the sort of wide social inequalities you would expect in an opportunity-driven society. Paul's correspondence suggests tensions between rich and poor were reflected within the Christian community, although most of those he recruited seem to have come from the lower echelons of society ("brothers and sisters: not many of you were wise by human standards, not many were powerful, not many were of noble birth," 1 Cor 1:26). It was religiously heterogeneous and lively—six of those members of the Corinthian church mentioned by name are explicitly said to have Jewish origins, but Paul's first letter indicates that most of the Corinthian Christians were converts from paganism ("You know that when you were pagans, you were enticed and lead astray to idols that could not speak," 1 Cor 12:2). It was also a community that welcomed refugees; the Acts of the Apostles says that the two converts who later became Paul's close confidants, Aquila and Priscilla, had fled to Corinth from an outbreak of anti-Jewish persecution in Rome. The sort of problems Paul dealt with in his correspondence suggests a Christian community and a wider society that were both in transition, with the rules being made up as everyone went along at a cracking pace. Even though Paul had rejected the Law, he had, as an observant Jew, been brought up in a world where the correct approach to absolutely every aspect of life was codified, and this kind of Wild West approach to ethics and social mores must have been deeply unsettling to him.

When Paul writes to the Corinthians he says, "I will stay in Ephesus until Pentecost" (1 Cor 16:8); it seems likely that the crisis in Corinth blew up at some point during the later part of his two years in Ephesus. And the news of trouble comes, as we have seen earlier, from "Chloe's people." One of the reasons Paul chose Ephesus as his center of operations was the excellent communications network it afforded him; Chloe is likely to have been an Ephesian businesswoman (in the Lydia mold), and when she sent a team of employees out to a city like Corinth it would have been natural for Paul to ask them to act as his informants. The exact sequence of the contacts with Corinth that their intelligence set in train is somewhat murky.

What in the New Testament canon is called Paul's First Letter to the Corinthians contains a reference to a previous correspondence ("I wrote to you in my letter not to associate with sexually immoral persons," 1 Cor 5:9), so it may be that we are coming in halfway through the conversation. The canonical Second Letter to the community at Corinth includes an intriguing suggestion of a visit there that does not feature in the Acts of the Apostles: "I call on God as witness against me: it was to spare you that I did not come again to Corinth.... I made up my mind not to make you *another painful visit*" (my italics, 2 Cor 1:23, 2:1). That seems to imply that at some point between writing the two canonical letters to the Corinthians, Paul left Ephesus to try to sort things out in Corinth in person but found himself caught up in an argument that may actually have made things worse. Another piece of the jigsaw is supplied by his reference to a so-called tearful letter: "I wrote to you out of much distress and anguish of heart and with many tears, not to cause you pain, but to let you know the abundant love that I have for you" (2 Cor 2:4). That letter has been lost to us, but if we put these scraps of evidence together it seems reasonable to suggest that Paul made a pastoral visit to Corinth that went horribly wrong, and followed it up with an angry, or "tearful," letter, designed to set things right. It would also appear that Paul sent an ambassador from Ephesus to Corinth early on in the drama. He recalls, "I sent you Timothy, who is my beloved and faithful child in the Lord, to remind you of my ways in Christ Jesus, as I teach them everywhere in every church" (1 Cor 4:17). Whatever the exact sequence of events, the contact between Paul and the community in Corinth was evidently intense and prolonged.

Paul gives us the key to understanding everything about his dispute with the Corinthians very early on in the canonical First Letter to the community; the disturbing news that comes with "Chloe's people" is that "there are quarrels among you, my brothers and sisters" (1 Cor 1:11). Paul's anxiety about divisions within the church provides the context for all the ethical guidance he goes on to lay out. The cause of discord in the Corinthian church seems to have been the Alexandrian Jew Apollos, who had earlier muddied the waters in Ephesus. Apollos features in both the Acts of the Apostles and the letters and he emerges as a somewhat ambiguous figure. He is described by St. Luke as "an eloquent man, well-versed in the scriptures. He had been instructed in the Way of the Lord; and he spoke with burning enthusiasm and taught accurately the things concerning Jesus" (Acts 18:24–25)—so he is certainly not condemned as a rival preacher like the Judaizers who challenged Paul's authority in the Galatian churches. Apollos's departure from orthodoxy came to light when Paul's old allies Priscilla and Aquila, who had gone to Ephesus ahead of him as an advance team, witnessed the Alexandrian preach in the synagogue. Not liking what they heard on the question of baptism, they "took him aside and explained the Way of God to him more accurately" (Acts 18:26). However, the conversation appears to have been amicably concluded (although this could of course be another example of Luke's spin), because Acts tells us that Apollos moved on to continue his mission in Corinth with their blessing, and they gave him letters of recommendation to the city's Christian community. At some stage Apollos must have returned to Ephesus to meet Paul face to face, because the First Letter to the Corinthians includes a reference to a conversation with "our brother Apollos" (1 Cor 16:12).

Quite what Apollos did in Corinth is not clear, but the impact of his mission there was an outbreak of factionalism:

> Each of you says, "I belong to Paul," or "I belong to Apollos," or "I belong to Cephas [Peter]," or "I belong to Christ." Has Christ been divided? Was Paul crucified for you? Or were you baptized in the name of Paul? I thank God that I baptized none of you except Crispus and Gaius, so that no one can say that you were baptized in my name. (1 Cor 1:12–15)

As the letter unfolds we get a picture of a Christian community that is not simply split over the preeminence of individual leaders—the church in Corinth was divided along every imaginable fault line, from diet to theology. Its members were suing one another in pagan courts: "When any of you has a grievance against another, do you dare to take it to court before the unrighteous, instead of taking it before the saints?" Paul demands in outrage (1 Cor 6:1). The old and endlessly divisive question of circumcision had come up, and Corinth's Christians had also fallen out over whether it was permissible to eat meat sacrificed to pagan idols. Some members of the community had become carried away with a sense of spiritual superiority, "puffed up in favor of one against another" (1 Cor 4:6), while others were anxious about their lowly social status ("Were you a slave when called? Do not be concerned about it," Paul writes reassuringly, 1 Cor 7:21). And the divisions within the community were coming into relief in an especially shameful way at precisely the occasion when they should have disappeared—at the celebration of the Eucharist. It seems that the Corinthian Christians would gather for a kind of group picnic before celebrating the Lord's Supper, and the social and economic differences within the community became all too apparent when everyone brought out their hampers: "For when the time comes to eat, each of you goes ahead with your own supper, and one goes hungry and another becomes drunk. What! Do you not have homes to eat and drink in? Or do you show contempt for the church of God and humiliate those who have nothing?" (1 Cor 11:21–22). For Paul these divisions undermine the very heart of the message of salvation he took to Corinth; "For as long as there is jealousy and quarreling among you, are you not of the flesh, and behaving according to human inclinations? For when one says, 'I belong to Paul,' and another, 'I belong to Apollos,' are you not merely human?" (1 Cor 3:3–4). The phrase "of the flesh" is a nuclear weapon of an insult in Paul's writing; it means worldly, pertaining to the darkness, lost to the light.

Paul reveals the genius of his religious imagination by the way he responds to the crisis in Corinth. From this unpromising cocktail of venality, pride, envy, and contention he forges two of Christianity's greatest poetic gifts to humanity—the hymn to love and the metaphor of the church as the body of Christ. In modern secular Britain the love hymn in 1 Corinthians 13 is probably better known than any other passage in the New Testament—if you are one of the many people who only ever go into a church for a wedding, this is the piece of scripture you are most likely to know:

125

If I speak in the tongues of mortals and of angels, but do not have love, I am a noisy gong or a clanging cymbal. And if I have prophetic powers, and understand all mysteries and all knowledge, and if I have all faith, so as to remove mountains, but do not have love, I am nothing. If I give away all my possessions, and if I hand over my body so that I may boast, but do not have love, I gain nothing.

Love is patient; love is kind; love is not envious or boastful or arrogant or rude. It does not insist on its own way; it is not irritable or resentful; it does not rejoice in wrongdoing, but rejoices in the truth. It bears all things, believes all things, hopes all things, endures all things.

Love never ends. But as for prophecies, they will come to an end; as for tongues, they will cease; as for knowledge, it will come to an end. For we know only in part, and we prophesy only in part; but when the complete comes, the partial will come to an end. When I was a child, I spoke like a child, I thought like a child, I reasoned like a child; when I became an adult, I put an end to childish ways. For now we see in a mirror, dimly, but then we will see face to face. Now I know only in part; then I will know fully, even as I have been fully known. And now faith, hope, and love abide, these three; and the greatest of these is love. (1 Cor 13:1–13)

There is a case for arguing that the use of this reading in so many wedding services represents yet another example of the way St. Paul's legacy is traduced by history. He is certainly not talking about romantic love, much less sexual desire; the Greek word *agape* means something more public and outward-looking than the word *love* as we understand it today in the context of a couple or even a nuclear family. Sometimes *agape* is translated as "charity," but that is somehow too dry and self-consciously virtuous a concept to convey what he is talking about. With that long list of "nots" Paul turns the negative tone of so much of this letter inside out, using everything that has gone wrong with the church in Corinth to define a Christian concept of agape in a very positive way. It is neither an entirely personal emotion nor an entirely public one; it is a spirit that should permeate both individual relationships between members of a Christian community and the bigger ties that bind the community as a whole. In this passage Paul really does pull off the trick of addressing a specific set of circumstances (in the course of the letter he goes through each of the areas that have proved a source of dissent meticulously and pragmatically), and, by the alchemy of language and imagination, turning the lesson they offer into something enduring. Tom Wright, the bishop of Durham and fully paid-up member of the Paul fan club, puts it like this:

> Paul builds up his argument step by step, showing at point after point the way in which this community is radically different from its pagan neighbours, until at last he reaches chapter 13, when, like the chorale theme in Sibelius' "Finlandia," the clear poetry in praise of love, *agape,* rings out, and we realize that this was all along the subtext of the entire letter…. Everything Paul has said so far on every topic has been, after all, an appeal for *agape.* This is the lifestyle that reveals what genuine renewed humanity is all about.

And it is precisely because St. Paul's agape is something more personal than charity and more public than romantic or sexual attraction that this passage of St. Paul does in fact work so effectively at occasions like weddings, when private and public feelings are both in play. The impact of the reading of the love hymn by the British Prime Minister, Tony Blair, at the funeral of Diana, Princess of Wales, provided a striking illustration of the way it can meet our need to participate in emotions that are bigger than ourselves without losing our sense of individuality.

The metaphor of the church as the body of Christ has less resonance in a post-Christian society like our own, but it has had a profound impact on the way Christianity has developed over the past two thousand years and, like the love hymn, it still has great poetic power today. It has often been invoked when Christianity has been threatened by schism, and was much quoted during the recent row within the Anglican Church over the issue of homo-sexuality. As its starting point it takes that idea in the Letter to the Galatians of a unity in Christ that transcends the old divisions of race, sex, and class, and then the metaphor uncurls itself through chapter 12 of the First Letter to the Corinthians like some theo-logical jazz riff—preparing the ground for the love hymn that immediately follows:

> For just as the body is one and has many members, and all the members of the body, though many, are one body, so it is with Christ. For in the one Spirit we were all baptized into one body—Jews or Greeks, slaves or free—and we were all made to drink of one Spirit.
>
> Indeed, the body does not consist of one member but of many. If the foot would say, "Because I am not a hand, I do not belong to the body," that would not make it any less a part of the body. And if the ear would say, "Because I am not an eye, I do not belong to the body," that would not make it any less a part of the body. If the whole body were an eye, where would the hearing be? If the whole of the body were hearing, where would the sense of smell be? But as it is, God arranged the members in the body, each one of them, as he chose. If all were a single member, where would the body be? As it is there are many members, yet one body. The eye cannot say to the hand, "I have no need of you," nor again the head to the feet, "I have no need of you." (1 Cor 12:12–21)

And so it goes on. The only way to get a real sense of the impact this passage must have had at the time is to perform the almost impossible feat of banishing two thousand years of assumptions about the nature of Jesus from your mind. Paul was writing to a group of people who had only recently been per-suaded that Jesus was the divine Son of God who had become man to save humankind, and he was telling them that they were part of his body. The church was a much less abstract concept then than it is now; it meant your friends and neighbors, perhaps your slaves and some of your enemies too. Paul was telling the Christians of Corinth that when they looked around those group picnics before the Eucharist they were looking at fellow members of the divine body. It is as compelling a rebuke for "quarrels" among them as it is possible to imagine.

In both these passages Paul is working more like a poet than a theologian or an ethicist, and the very specific ethical advice and instruction he gives in the course of the First Letter to the Corinthians has to be seen in that context. The inspired religious insights expressed in the love hymn and the metaphor of the church as the body of Christ are the really enduring legacies of his correspondence with the church—his rulings on such matters as divorce, adultery, and long-haired men are footnotes to those central texts. The point is brought home by the way he treats the question of eating food that has been sacrificed to idols. Paul's advice is entirely pragmatic: those who know that idols do not really exist as gods need not trouble themselves about the issue, because they understand that it is a dilemma posited on false beliefs; but they must equally be careful not to confuse less well-informed members of the church who may not be as sure in their minds about whether idols do or do not have some kind of spiritual status. To Paul it matters not a jot whether Christians eat food that has been sacrificed to idols, but he cares very much about a community bound together by agape.

He is certainly not anti-sex. There is a clear distinction between the way he uses the word *flesh* and the way he uses the word *body*. The flesh means carnality in its basest sense, and is associated with the dark powers that dominate unsaved humankind. The body is, as we have seen, associated with Christ, and toward the end of chapter 12 of the First Letter to the Corinthians the extended metaphor of the church as the body of Christ takes a slightly surprising turn:

> those members of the body that seem to be weaker are indispensable, and those members of the body that we think less honorable we clothe with greater honor, and our less respectable members are treated with greater

respect; whereas our more respectable members do not need this. But God has so arranged the body, giving the greater honor to the inferior member, that there may be no dissension within the body, but the members may have the same care for one another. (1 Cor 12:22–25)

I cannot read this without feeling that Paul was not particularly enthusiastic about his "less respectable" and "inferior" member, but his theology of the body does produce a very humane teaching about marriage:

The husband should give to his wife her conjugal rights, and likewise the wife to her husband. For the wife does not have authority over her own body, but the husband does; likewise the husband does not have authority over his own body, but the wife does. Do not deprive one another except perhaps by agreement for a set time, to devote yourselves to prayer, and then come together again, so that Satan may not tempt you because of your lack of self-control. (1 Cor 7:3–5).

That last sentence may seem to suggest that sex in marriage is simply a means of avoiding the sin of fornication, but Paul's central idea of a couple exercising joint sovereignty over one another's bodies is surely positive and life-enhancing.

There is of course another side to the close identification of Christ with the body. "The body is meant not for fornication but for the Lord, and the Lord for the body.... Do you not know that your bodies are members of Christ? Should I therefore take the members of Christ and make them members of a prostitute? Never! Do you not know that whoever is united to a prostitute becomes one body with her?" (1 Cor 6:13, 15–16) Sex that Paul disapproves of becomes doubly disgusting to him because he believes in a mystical union between Christ and the members of his church. Plainly Paul condemned prostitution, and it seems to me that despite all the attempts to soften his position on same-sex relationships he was uncompromisingly opposed to homosexuality too. It is a source of another of those Pauline paradoxes; I have tried to argue that all of Paul's ethical teaching needs to be seen in the context of his overriding passion for the integrity of a Christian community united by agape; yet his views on homosexuality are today at the heart of exactly the kind of divisions and factions that caused him such anxiety when he saw them develop in the Corinthian church.

There are two references in his letters to homosexual behavior. In the First Letter to the Corinthians it is dismissed in an almost offhand way as simply one item on the list of condemned practices that I quoted at the beginning of this chapter. Much more direct is the second passage on the subject in his Letter to the Romans:

> Their women exchanged natural intercourse for unnatural, and in the same way also the men, giving up natural intercourse with women, were consumed with passion for one another. Men committed shameless acts with men and received in their own persons the due penalty for their error.
>
> And since they did not see fit to acknowledge God, God gave them up to a debased mind and to things that should not be done. (Rom 1:26–28)

This passage comes in the course of a much wider description of the way the world is turned on its head when humankind abandons God for idol worship and "exchange[s] the truth about God for a lie" (Rom 1:25). At an intellectual level Paul clearly believed that homosexual acts were a perversion of the order of things ordained by God, a distortion of the God-given relationship between male and female. Homosexual love had of course been a salient characteristic of classical Greek culture—not merely tolerated but actively encouraged in some societies—and Dr. Sanders told me that the amount of homoerotic art that has been found on Roman lamps and plates and in their wall paintings suggests it was still a significant factor in the Roman Corinth of Paul's time. By attacking something that was widely accepted in the society around him Paul was, his champions argue, simply showing himself to be true to his Jewish origins. "He's trotting out the typical condemnations towards the Gentiles," Father Scott Brodeur explained. "The Jews were very proud in antiquity of their faith in the Lord and they were also very proud of the fact that their behavior, especially their sexual behavior, set them apart from the pagans. Under the Law homosexuality was not allowed and Paul was simply being faithful to that."

But of course Paul preached freedom from the Law, and the cultural context of the first century is not quite enough to lay the debate about his attitude to homosexuality to rest. Because he is a poet as much as a theologian his feelings come through his writing as clearly as his ideas; his opposition to gay sex—male and female—seems visceral to me, and the passage from the Letter to the Romans quoted above conveys a shiver of almost physical disgust as well as moral condemnation. There is a school of thought that suggests that the violence of his emotions on the subject springs from the suppression of his own sexuality, and that Paul was himself homosexual. That, the theory goes, explains what he means when, in a notoriously mysterious passage of the Second Letter to the Corinthians, he says "to keep me from being too elated, a thorn was given me in the flesh, a messenger of Satan to torment me" (2 Cor 12:7). The affection Paul expressed for the slave Onesimus in his Letter to Philemon ("my child, Onesimus, whose father I have become during my imprisonment" Phlm 10) is sometimes cited as further evidence for a gay St. Paul. John Shelby Spong, famous for championing liberal causes during his time as Episcopal bishop of Newark, New Jersey, has argued: "The war that went on between what he [Paul] desired with his mind and what he desired with his body, his drivenness to a legalistic religion of control, his fear when that system was threatened, his attitude towards women, his refusal to seek marriage as an outlet for his passion—nothing else accounts for this data as well as the possibility that Paul was gay."

It is, of course, an impossible proposition to verify or to refute. The Christian gay rights group Changing Attitudes points out that Paul writes of homosexual behavior as a matter of "free and perverse choice, whereas we now understand that for most gay people there is no choice in the matter at all." At the risk of anachronism, I would suggest that means he probably did not understand homosexuality "from the inside," but the honest truth is that we simply do not have enough evidence to make a definitive statement one way or another. What is beyond doubt is the pain that has been caused to gay and lesbian Christians by the way Paul's views on homosexuality have been interpreted. The director of Changing Attitudes, the Reverend Colin Coward, is a psychotherapist as well as an Anglican priest, and believes it has encouraged "in lesbian and gay people themselves a really horrendous self judgementalism, anxiety about the self and often a deeply internalised disgust which has been incredibly damaging."

What would Paul think of the current debate in the Anglican Communion about homosexuality? It is an enticing question because of the way his name is so often brandished about by the conservative opponents of gay bishops, and it goes to the heart of the issue of the status we accord Paul's letters. To try to minimize the depth of his opposition to homosexual acts does violence to the truth; it is woven into his theology, it is integral to his cultural and religious background, and it is felt in his gut. There is, however, one further factor that is critical to any assessment of Paul's moral teachings; his belief in what is technically called *parousia*, the Second Coming of Christ. "The appointed time has grown short," he writes to the Corinthians, "the present form of this world is passing away" (1 Cor 7:29, 31). The sense that some kind of apocalypse is approaching lends a provisional feeling to much of his moral teaching. He is evidently confident about the big points of principle ("Love never ends"), but much less so about their practical implications. "Now concerning virgins," he writes somewhat tentatively, "I have no command of the Lord, but I give my opinion as one who by the Lord's mercy is trustworthy. I think that, in view of the impending crisis [Christ's Second Coming], it is well for you to remain as you are" (1 Cor 7:25–26). Paul's instructions sometimes seem to be not so much immutable rules as ad hoc suggestions for getting through the relatively short interlude before the arrival of the kingdom of heaven.

I am not sure there is an intellectually respectable solution to this conundrum. A liberal argument (Paul did not really mean what he said about gay people and was speaking only as a man of his time) simply does not square with the facts. A rigorously conservative argument (this is scripture and these teachings cannot be tampered with) contradicts itself. If everything in Paul's letters is to be taken as literal, absolute and eternal truth, the idea of imminent parousia must be accepted as fully as the teaching on homosexuality; that implies Paul believed the world was about to end, so he cannot have thought that he was laying down rules that would endure until the twenty-first century. The idea that we "know" where God stands in this argument is hubristic in the extreme. I find myself falling back, in a thoroughly unscientific way, on my instincts about what sort of a man Paul was. He was fierce and passionate, and sometimes sarcastic, but he was not cruel. I feel sure that Paul would have been touched by the suffering of those who have been unable to reconcile his teaching with their own natures. During the public debate about homosexuality in the Church of England I interviewed an elderly bishop on the *Today* program who had "come out" in his retirement. He said he had finally decided that Paul was simply wrong about homosexuality, but it had taken him years of soul searching to reach that conclusion. Paul would surely have been impressed by the sincerity of the many Christians who have gone through the same painful process. This is, of course, no more than my instinct, and a hopelessly speculative conclusion to an argument that can probably never be settled.

Women, like gays, have suffered in the shadow of St. Paul's ethical teaching. The essayist and novelist Marina Warner has written an elegiac account of being taught about the apostle by the nuns at an English Catholic boarding school hidden in the rhododendrons of the Home Counties. She says she became a "house divided against itself" because she so much admired the stories of Paul's adventurous life, but at the same time felt consigned to the role of silent, second-class citizen by his views on women:

> Enclosed at school, we were immobilised, and very far away from the heart of things. He enjoyed intimacy with the Lord, and all that meant in terms of power and love and light; we sat at our desks facing the blackboard in classrooms with high windows so that the view outside would not distract us, journeying with Paul on his

many roads, by land and sea, along lines of green and red ballpoint. In the fifth form (aged about 15) we could bicycle with permission to the local village beyond the shrubs and birch trees, but never farther afield. It was important to learn the love of Christ by sitting still and being good; Paul dynamic, adventurous Paul to whom so much had happened, was the architect of this view of girls' proper conduct.

But was he? I find much of the evidence that is usually cited for Paul's male chauvinism unconvincing. His instruction to the Corinthians that women should wear a veil in church has traditionally been taken as proof that he regarded women as inherently inferior to men. Margaret Thrall, a Lecturer in Biblical Studies at the University of North Wales writing in the 1960s, put it like this: "To Paul it was important because it symbolized an attitude of mind to which he objected. When the Corinthian women discarded their veils this was a conscious attempt to assert their equality with the men in the congregation. Paul argues that, on the contrary, women are by nature subordinate to men." In fact Paul follows the instruction about veils with a remarkably original and direct statement that the Genesis story of Adam and Eve cannot be taken to mean that man is superior to woman: "in the Lord woman is not independent of man or man independent of woman. For just as woman came from man, so man comes through woman; but all things come from God" (1 Cor 11:11–12).

There is a more problematic passage in the same letter where Paul says that women should "be silent in the churches" and declares, "If there is anything they desire to know, let them ask their husbands at home" (1 Cor 14:34–35). Father Jerome Murphy O'Connor, a great champion of a "feminist" Paul, states flatly that this "cannot come from the pen of Paul" and was added at a later date by an editor seeking to impose his own views on the apostle's writing; his case is lent some force by the fact that Paul does allow for the idea of women speaking in church elsewhere in the letter. But even if we accept these as Paul's own words, they can surely be excused to some degree by the cultural context of his time. They do, after all, address matters of decorum and manners rather than theological truth.

The passage relating to the role of women for which Paul is most frequently condemned comes not in his First Letter to the Corinthians, but in one of the so-called pastoral epistles, 1 Timothy:

> I desire, then, that in every place the men should pray, lifting up holy hands without anger or argument; also that the women should dress themselves modestly and decently in suitable clothing, not with hair braided, or with gold, pearls, or expensive clothes, but with good works, as is proper for women who profess reverence for God. Let a woman learn in silence with full submission. I permit no woman to teach or to have authority over a man; she is to keep silent. For Adam was formed first, then Eve; and Adam was not deceived, but the woman was deceived and became a transgressor. Yet she will be saved through childbearing, provided they continue in faith and love and holiness, with modesty. (1 Tim 2:8–15)

The overwhelming scholarly consensus is that the pastoral letters were not the work of Paul, but were written some decades later (probably around the end of the first century or in the early years of the second) by an anonymous author who may have been in some way associated with the circle of his disciples. As C. J. Den Heyer puts it: "In language and style these letters differ so much from the other letters which are attributed to the apostle that it is difficult to imagine how they all came from one and the same pen." And it is clear from the content of the pastoral letters that the church has developed into something much closer to an institution by the time they were written; 1 Timothy, for example, includes a lengthy dissertation on the appropriate lifestyle for deacons and bishops. Of all the many injustices done to Paul this may be the worst; he simply did not write the words that have been used to do so much harm in his name.

Paul's genuine letters are full of affectionate greetings to women whom he clearly valued. Even more importantly, taken together the letters and the Acts of the Apostles suggest he emphatically rejected the view that no woman should be allowed "to teach or to have authority over a man." He was obviously happy to accept and indeed to embrace the independence of women like Lydia and Chloe, and in his Letter to the Romans he refers to one Phoebe as "a deacon of the church" (Rom 16:1). The question of whether Paul would have approved of women priests is as anachronistic and unanswerable as the question of whether he was gay, but my instinct is that he would have approved.

The boil of Paul's troubled relationship with the Corinthian church seems to have been lanced when he sent Titus, another of his aides, as his ambassador to the city, perhaps bearing that mysterious "tearful letter" with him. Paul left Ephesus without knowing the outcome of this mission, and sailed back across the Aegean to Europe. At some point as he worked his way across Greece to visit Corinth for the last time, he met Titus coming the other way with good news; the Corinthians had accepted Paul's guidance and authority. Part of the Second Letter to the Corinthians, written after this meeting, reveals a Paul in altogether more cheerful spirits: "we rejoiced still more at the joy of Titus, because his mind has been set at rest by all of you.... And his heart goes out all the more to you, as he remembers the obedience of all of you, and how you welcomed him in fear and trembling. I rejoice, because I have complete confidence in you" (2 Cor 7:13, 15–16).

8

Paul, Man of Two Worlds

Paul was brooding during those final months of his third missionary journey. The news that Titus brought him from Corinth may have cheered him up as he crossed Greece for the last time, but there are passages in the Second Letter to the Corinthians that read like the thoughts of a man in a midlife crisis. It is the least "theological"—in the abstract sense—of his substantial letters, and it begins with what one can only describe as whining: "We do not want you to be unaware, brothers and sisters, of the affliction we experienced in Asia; for we were so utterly, unbearably crushed that we despaired of life itself" (2 Cor 1:8). At times it is almost as if he is talking to himself rather than the Corinthians, trying to bolster his own conviction that the extraordinary task he has set himself (or, as he would of course see it, that God has set for him) is worthwhile: "We are afflicted in every way," he declares, "but not crushed; perplexed, but not driven to despair; persecuted, but not forsaken; struck down, but not destroyed; always carrying in the body the death of Jesus, so that the life of Jesus may also be made visible in our bodies" (2 Cor 4:8–10). That last idea is both striking and difficult, but if we put Christology to one side for a moment Paul stands before us as a man who has hit middle age and is feeling it:

> Even though our outer nature is wasting away, our inner nature is being renewed day by day. For this slight momentary affliction is preparing us for an eternal weight of glory beyond all measure, because we look not at what can be seen but at what cannot be seen; for

what can be seen is temporary, but what cannot be seen
is eternal. (2 Cor 4:16–18)

Does he protest too much? Could it—and I hesitate to ask this—
be that the apostle himself suffered a moment of doubt about
"what cannot be seen"? Perhaps that is reading too much into the
text.

But Paul is clearly fed up with the continued sniping of his
rivals. The dramatic declaration of what he has gone through in
the course of his missionary journeys—which I quoted at the
beginning of chapter 5—is part of an extraordinary passage when
he really lets fly at the competition:

> But whatever anyone dares to boast of—I am speaking
> as a fool—I also dare to boast of that. Are they
> Hebrews? So am I. Are they Israelites? So am I. Are
> they descendants of Abraham? So am I. Are they min-
> isters of Christ? I am talking like a madman—I am a
> better one: with far greater labors, far more imprison-
> ments, with countless floggings, and often near death.
> (2 Cor 11:21–23)

This is a man giving full rein to bitter feelings.

Paul is thought to have arrived in Corinth himself late in the
year, and he wintered there for three months at the end of his
third missionary journey. He was surrounded by friends; he stayed
with Gaius—evidently a figure of some substance in the community, because Paul refers to him as "my host and host to the whole
church"—and enjoyed the company of Timothy, his "co-worker,"
Lucius, Jason, and Sosipater (whom he describes as "my compa-
triots" or, more intriguingly, according to some translations, "my
relatives") and a group of other Christians including "the city
treasurer" Erastus (Rom 16:21–23). In the course of this stay
Paul produced what is generally regarded as the crowning glory
of his thought, the Letter to the Romans—an achievement
described by Samuel Taylor Coleridge as simply "the most profound work in existence." On the face of it the contrast between
this Letter and the Second Letter to the Corinthians (which was

written only a few months earlier) could not be greater; if 2 Corinthians is the least theological and the most personal of the letters, Romans is the opposite—a tsunami of abstract argument, scriptural exegesis, mysticism, and polemic crashing through sixteen tempestuous chapters. What had happened between the composition of the two letters?

Luke provides us with only the sparsest of outlines of Paul's movements during this period. He despatches him from Ephesus and completes his account of this stage of Paul's third missionary journey in two brief sentences: "Paul sent for the disciples; and after encouraging them and saying farewell, he left for Macedonia. When he had gone through those regions and had given the believers much encouragement, he came to Greece, where he stayed for three months" (Acts 20:1–3). To make up for Luke's uncharacteristic taciturnity, I am going to break all my own rules about rigorous journalistic skepticism and allow myself a fantasy at this point—it is a relatively harmless one and I find it a helpful way to ease myself into the dense tangle of ideas and action that make up the final stages of Paul's public life.

Corinth in the winter can be a bleak place; if you make the steep climb to the top of the acropolis you are quite likely to face the kind of conditions usually associated with the North Yorkshire Moors rather than the Mediterranean. I am going to allow myself to picture Paul, with the winter wind in his hair and the rain at his back, striding across the cliff top and conducting an internal audit of his achievements and his prospects—the kind of soul-searching and stocktaking that you might expect in someone going through their midlife crisis.

He is now well into his fifties. The parousia he has been expecting and longing for has failed to materialize, so clearly the conviction that "time is short," which drove him on his first visit here, needs some revision. And the view before him encourages him to think of his life at a crossroads; to the east, across the Aegean, lie Asia Minor, Antioch, Damascus, and Jerusalem, and a past rich with incident; to the west, across the Adriatic, lie Rome, the capital of the empire, and, perhaps even more enticingly, the virgin mission fields of Spain beyond.

If we pause for a moment with Paul as he looks east and reviews his career to date, we are forced to conclude that this iconic Christian hero was an inveterate, and apparently incurable troublemaker. His recent departure from Ephesus, for example, had been provoked by a riot of the city's silversmiths, who felt that his proselytizing was damaging their lucrative trade in statues of the goddess Artemis (it is one of St. Luke's most vivid set pieces, and the silversmiths' meeting in the great theater of Ephesus seems to have been really quite a serious threat to civil order). And somewhere beyond the storm clouds on the horizon lies a prison cell with which Paul is all too familiar. He almost certainly did time during the couple of years he spent in Ephesus; there is compelling internal evidence that both the Letter to the Philippians and the Letter to Philemon were written while he was a prisoner there, and his imprisonment may well be the "affliction we experienced in Asia" he refers to in the Second Letter to the Corinthians.

As he gazes inland toward Athens, he remembers that first European missionary journey, when in almost every city along the way he found himself caught up in a ruckus of some kind or another, and of course did another brief spell behind bars in Philippi. Even Corinth, spread below him at the foot of the cliff, stirs memories of past troubles; on his first visit here the city's Jews hauled him up before the proconsul, Gallio, and accused him of "persuading people to worship God in ways that are contrary to the law" (Acts 18:13).

All of this comes flooding back to Paul as he surveys the panorama before him. Given the profoundly revolutionary nature of his apocalyptic message it is scarcely surprising that it has caused trouble. What could be more provocative than turning up in a city and announcing that the established order of things is about to be turned on its head? Those with a vested interest in the status quo—the silversmiths in Ephesus, the synagogue officials in Corinth, the owners of the prophesying slave in Philippi—were bound to react badly. But the fact that his difficulties were predictable does not make them easier to bear—and as he reflects on what his achievements have cost him, the taunts of the rivals that provoked that outburst in the Second Letter to the Corinthians sting him again with renewed bitterness. If he felt a yearning for a more tranquil future, who can blame him? Metaphorically shaking the dust of the east from his shoes, Paul turns and strides across the bluff, turning his eyes westward—toward Rome, and a new adventure.

With Paul's decision to visit Rome, we can leave my mountaintop fantasy behind and come down to earth again, because the evidence suggests that the idea did indeed take shape during his winter in Corinth. He had been thinking about it for some time; St. Luke says that while he was still based in Ephesus he declared, "I must also see Rome" (Acts 19:21). And when he writes to the Romans to introduce himself he similarly suggests that this has been a project long in the making: "God, whom I serve with my spirit by announcing the gospel of his Son, is my witness that without ceasing I remember you always in my prayers, asking that by God's will I may somehow at last succeed in coming to you. For I am longing to see you so that I may share with you some spiritual gift to strengthen you" (Rom 1:9–11). If we accept the fact that Paul was as proud of his Roman citizenship as Luke suggests, a pilgrimage to the Eternal City would have been a natural ambition.

Paul's own explanation of why he took the decision to make the journey at this moment in his career is intriguing. The origins of Roman Christianity are lost—tradition says the faith was brought to the heart of the empire by St. Peter, but we have no evidence to indicate when or how that might have happened. However, the church was evidently well established there by the time Paul wrote his Letter to the Romans. Paul says he has always preferred to evangelize new territory, and there is a hint in the letter that he is sensitive to the charge of poaching on someone else's patch (we know how raw he feels about rival Christian missionaries who poach on his):

> Thus I make it my ambition to proclaim the good news, not where Christ has already been named, so that I do not build on someone else's foundation, but, as it is written,

"Those who have never been told of him shall see,
and those who have never heard of him shall
understand."
This is the reason that I have so often been hin-
dered from coming to you. (Rom 15:20–21)

Even at this stage he seems reluctant to propose anything as
formal as a missionary journey to Rome, almost as if he fears that
the idea would be regarded as somehow presumptuous. Instead
he says he will drop in on the city "when I go to Spain." But most
intriguing of all is this: "But now, with no further place for me in
these regions, I desire, as I have for many years, to come to you"
(Rom 15:23–24). What does Paul mean when he says there is "no
further place for me in these regions"? He can surely not be suggesting that he has done all the evangelizing he can in the eastern
Mediterranean. Perhaps my fantasy picture of a Paul feeling weary
and stale and in need of a fresh start is not so very far from the
truth.

The Letter to the Romans has traditionally been regarded as
different in kind from Paul's other letters. All of those I have discussed so far were written to individuals and communities well
known to Paul; they were, as we have seen, generally composed
with a particular set of problems or events in mind, so their theology is, to use a piece of scholarly jargon, "contextual." When
Paul wrote to the Romans, however, he was addressing an
unknown audience; since he had never been to Rome—so the
argument runs—he could not have understood the particular circumstances of the church there, and we must therefore regard the
theology of this letter in a different way. It is abstract, not contextual, and in the Letter to the Romans Paul, according to this view,
consciously set out to produce his theological last will and testament. "It has beyond any other of St Paul's epistles," wrote
Charles Gore, Canon at Westminster Abbey and chaplain to the
Queen, in the 1890s, "the character of an ordered theological
treatise.... He is in writing it committing to the future the fruits
of his labours, so far as they can be expressed in a doctrine."

It only requires a moment or two's reflection to realize what
a very odd thing that would have been for Paul to do. His belief

in the imminence of the Second Coming makes it most unlikely that he would have thought it worth his while to leave any kind of theological legacy at all, and even if he had he would surely have entrusted it to one of his close associates—Timothy, after all, was staying with him in Corinth—rather than sending it off to a place he had never seen. In fact the Letter to the Romans had a practical purpose in exactly the way that all Paul's letters do: it was a way of introducing himself to the community in Rome and preparing them for his visit.

One modern scholar has rather ingeniously suggested that you can only really understand the Letter to the Romans by reading it backward; the final chapter includes greetings to nearly thirty individuals and an undefined number of "brothers and sisters" and families (there is a school that argues that this chapter of the Letter to the Romans is in fact part of a separate letter addressed to the Ephesians, but since the controversy has been rumbling on since the eighteenth century without any sign of a resolution I feel at liberty to ignore it). Paul may not have been to Rome at this stage, but he certainly seems to have known plenty of members of the Roman church, and it therefore seems likely that when he sat down to write the Letter to the Romans he was able to draw on extensive intelligence about what was happening there.

The two names at the top of his greetings list are especially significant. Prisca (Priscilla) and Aquila—Diaspora Jewish converts like Paul—had become his close confidants—we last met them acting as his advance party in Ephesus, and Paul says they had "risked their necks for my life" (Rom 16:3–4). Working on the Letter to the Romans during his stay in Corinth, he will surely have remembered the circumstances of his first meeting with the couple in the same city. St. Luke says that they had fled to Corinth from Italy "because Claudius had ordered all Jews to leave Rome" (Acts 18:2). The historian Suetonius records that the emperor Claudius expelled the Jews from Rome because they were causing "continuous disturbances at the instigation of Chrestus." The temptation to see *Chrestus* as a corruption of *Christ* is irresistible, and if we put those two bits of evidence together it seems reasonable to propose that there was some form of trouble involving

Roman Christians (probably in the late 40s) that led to a general punishment of the city's Jews (the authorities could be forgiven for finding it difficult to distinguish between Judaism and Christianity at this stage).

By the time Paul wrote the Letter to the Romans, Claudius was dead and Priscilla and Aquila were back in Rome. But their account of what it was like to be driven out of their home must have made a strong impression on Paul—they had plenty of time to chat in the hours they spent stitching away during their partnership in the tentmaking business—and if it was on his mind during the composition of Romans, it would at least help to explain one of the letter's most problematic passages:

> Let every person be subject to the governing authorities; for there is no authority except from God, and those authorities that exist have been instituted by God. Therefore whoever resists authority resists what God has appointed, and those who resist will incur judgment. For rulers are not a terror to good conduct, but to bad. (Rom 13:1–3)

This endorsement of Roman imperial rule has given comfort to monarchs, dictators, and all manner of unpleasant political regimes down the centuries. It was the foundation stone of the doctrine of the Divine Right of Kings that caused such mayhem in seventeenth- and eighteenth-century Europe, it helped to salve the consciences of those Christians who supported the Nazi regime in Germany, and provided a cloak of Pauline respectability for apartheid in South Africa too. It seems particularly surprising from the pen of a man who clearly enjoyed a good argument and had a proven track record as a troublemaker. But if we treat this passage as simply a piece of advice written with the unpleasant experience suffered by Priscilla and Aquila during the Claudian expulsion in mind, it makes some kind of sense.

By and large, Paul's experience of Roman authority had been positive. A decade later the emperor Nero was to prove his proposition that "rulers are not a terror to good conduct, but to bad" spectacularly wrong with his savage anti-Christian persecutions, but as Paul looked around him in the prosperous Roman colony of Corinth he would have been struck first and foremost by the many benefits of a stable society under a strong central authority. The image we have of him as a troublemaker can be misleading; despite the riots and the run-ins with entrenched interests during his earlier missionary journeys, the imperial Roman bureaucracy seems until now to have been remarkably untroubled by Paul's activities. When the Jews of Corinth hauled Paul before the pro-consul, for example, Gallio swats away their charges with haughty Roman disdain: "Since it is a matter of questions about words and names and your own law, see to it yourselves; I do not wish to be a judge of these matters" (Acts 18:15). We do have to be a little wary of Luke's evidence in this area; one of his objectives in writing the Acts of the Apostles may have been to persuade a skeptical Roman audience of the late first century that the new religion putting down roots in their midst should not necessarily be seen as a threat, and Luke no doubt doctored his account of Paul's encounters with Roman authority accordingly. However, there is nothing in Paul's own letters to suggest that—Roman citizen that he apparently was—he regarded a political challenge to Roman authority as part of his mission.

Plenty of other Jews at this period were actively trying to ferment rebellion against Rome. Hyam Maccoby argues that Jesus himself was essentially a peaceful political revolutionary who was crucified because he posed a challenge to the imperial authorities in Jerusalem. And this was the age of the Sicarii, the Jewish terrorists who dedicated themselves to the assassination of anyone who collaborated with Roman rule (they took their name from the small daggers, or *sicae,* that they kept hidden beneath their cloaks). Paul played on a world stage, and the man who declared that "there is no Jew or Greek" is unlikely to have been attracted by the political cause of nationalism. His targets were Satan and sin, not Rome and its colonial power.

And perhaps this middle-aged man was beginning to feel the seductive pull of a less confrontational style of life. Paul's views on civil authority, contentious though they have proved, are merely a footnote to the great themes of his Letter to the Romans: salvation, righteousness, and the nature of God's promises to humankind. As so often, the big theological questions are framed in terms of the relationship between Jewish and Gentile Christianity. Until now this topic has been relentlessly raw in Paul's writing, but many commentators have remarked on the way Paul's approach suddenly mellows. The judgment of Albert Schweitzer, the German theologian who went on to win a Nobel Prize for his missionary work, is typical: "All polemic against the apostles in Jerusalem is avoided," he writes, "and his attachment to his ancestral race is emphasized to the utmost." The sarcasm with which Paul rips into the Judaizers in his earlier letters has gone, and in its place there is an almost elegiac tenderness for what Judaism represents.

At one level this is simply emotional, reflecting the natural nostalgia of a man in his fifties for a childhood faith left behind:

> I have great sorrow and unceasing anguish in my heart. For I could wish that I myself were accursed and cut off from Christ for the sake of my own people, my kindred according to the flesh. They are Israelites, and to them belong the adoption, the glory, the covenants, the giving of the law, the worship, and the promises; to them belong the patriarchs, and from them, according to the flesh, comes the Messiah, who is over all, God blessed forever. Amen. (Rom 9:2–5)

Paul's pride in the spiritual blue blood he can claim as a Jew shines through, and he deftly draws his Messiah, Jesus, into the tradition of Judaism as if it is the most natural thing imaginable. In the opening preamble to this letter, the Apostle to the Gentiles declares where his heart lies: "For I am not ashamed of the gospel; it is the power of God for salvation to everyone who has faith," he declares "*to the Jew first* and also to the Greek" (my italics, Rom 1:16).

But Paul is not only reflecting a change in himself—he is also recognizing a change in the objective reality of the church he has done so much to establish. The Princeton scholar J. Ross Wagner pictures this pivotal moment like this: "Paul is painfully aware of the growing paradox of the early Christian mission; while Gentiles joyfully receive the Gospel in ever growing numbers, it is becoming increasingly apparent that the majority of Paul's fellow Jews are not finding his message to be 'good news.'" Paul's earlier letters on this subject—notably his Letter to the Galatians—were written under intense pressure from the partisans of the Law; he is now writing as one who is winning the argument. The freedom from the sense that he is vulnerable to constant challenges to his authority takes some of the sting out of his rhetoric, and with the new reality represented by the Roman church in mind he allows the pendulum of his thinking to swing back toward his Jewish roots.

It is often argued that the ascendancy of the Gentile element in the church was especially marked in the Roman Christian community he was addressing; because of the Claudian expulsion of the Jews from Rome, Gentile Christians there may have been able to put their stamp on Christianity much more forcefully there than they did elsewhere. It would certainly seem that Paul expected Gentile Christians to be the primary recipients of the Letter to the Romans; in the great rolling opening sentence (you have to get through nearly 130 words before you hit a period), he speaks of his task "to bring about the obedience of faith among all the Gentiles for the sake of his name, *including yourselves* who are called to belong to Jesus Christ" (my italics, Rom 1:5–6), and a little later he says he is coming to Rome "in order that I may reap some harvest among you as I have among the rest of the Gentiles" (Rom 1:13). And where in past letters he has been trying to protect Gentile Christians from the obligation to submit themselves to circumcision and the Law, in this letter he is asking them to be sensitive to the feelings of their Jewish co-religionists by, for example, respecting the importance of their customs on diet. He pleads:

> Let us therefore not pass judgment on one another, but resolve instead never to put a stumbling block or hindrance in the way of another. I know and am persuaded in the Lord Jesus that nothing is unclean in itself; but it is unclean for anyone who thinks it unclean. If your brother or sister is being injured by what you eat, you are no longer walking in love. (Rom 14:13–15)

All of this is part of a new twist to the purpose of Paul's mission: "Now I am speaking to you Gentiles. Inasmuch then as I am an apostle to the Gentiles, I glorify my ministry in order to make my own people jealous, and thus save some of them" (Rom 11:13–14). Paul's efforts to bring the good news to the Gentiles have become a means to a different end—saving the Jewish people too.

Paul's theological argument for the salvation of the Jews is worked through with the depth of scriptural learning one would expect from the Pharisee who "advanced in Judaism beyond many among my people of the same age" (Gal 1:14). The Letter to the Romans is stuffed with quotation from and allusion to the Old Testament—the whole of chapter 4 is dedicated to a new interpretation of the Abraham story, and chapters 9, 10, and 11 are crammed with references to Genesis, Exodus, Leviticus, Deuteronomy, the Psalms, and, above all, Isaiah. Paul reworks the old texts to explain the rejection of Christ by the Jews, to give a new meaning to his own mission as a bridge between Jews and Gentiles, and to prophesy the eventual salvation of the Jewish people. The Gentiles will be saved first and the Jews will follow: "a hardening has come upon part of Israel, until the full number of the Gentiles has come in" (Rom 11:25), and Paul's mission is to play a pivotal role in the unfolding of this providential process. As J. Ross Wagner puts it:

> By adopting as his own the stories Isaiah and his fellow scriptural witnesses tell about God's unquenchable love for his people, Paul is able to maintain confidently that the God who is now embracing the Gentiles as his own will be faithful to redeem and restore his covenant people Israel as well, so that Jew and Gentile can with one voice laud the incomparable mercy of their God.

As he makes his case Paul is quite explicit in the way he encourages Gentile Christians to use the Old Testament as a source of enlightenment: "For whatever was written in former days was written for our instruction" (Rom 15:4), he says. So the Paul who is so often condemned as the father of Christian anti-Semitism is also the Paul who, in the Letter to the Romans, gave birth to the notion that the traditions of Judaism are treasures that the Christian church must preserve. Over the past thirty years or so there has been an academic campaign to "rescue" Paul from the idea that his theology was dedicated to the destruction of Judaism. The new orthodoxy is expressed by James Dunn of Durham University like this: "His message to Christians is that Christianity is in some sense a form of Judaism, or a continuation of the religion of Israel, and cannot understand itself unless it understands itself in those terms. It's simply a fact that two thirds of the contents of the Christian bible are the sacred writings of Jews." Reassuringly, the Paul we have come to know and enjoy does not entirely disappear in all this harmonious mellowness; even as he urges his audience to "Bless those who persecute you; bless and do not curse them" (Rom 12:14), there is a flash of the old controversialist; "if your enemies are hungry, feed them; if they are thirsty, give them something to drink; for by doing this you will be heaping burning coals on their heads" (Rom 12:20–21).

Paul characteristically finds a practical hook on which to hang his latest theological garments. Before he can realize his dream to go to Rome and Spain he must first fulfill a promise he made to James and Peter at the conclusion of the Jerusalem Council: "They asked only one thing, that we remember the poor, which was actually what I was eager to do" (Gal 2:10). The collection on behalf of the poor of Jerusalem has preoccupied Paul during the months leading up to his stay in Corinth, and in his Letter to the Romans it reemerges as a symbol of the complex relationship between Judaism and Gentile Christianity he has developed in the letter. "I do hope to see you on my journey and to be sent on by you," he writes as the great theological crescendos of the letter give way to calmer and more practical waters:

> At present, however, I am going to Jerusalem in a ministry to the saints; for Macedonia and Achaia have been pleased to share their resources with the poor among the saints at Jerusalem. They were pleased to do this, and indeed they owe it to them; for if the Gentiles have

come to share their spiritual blessings, they ought also to be of service to them in material things. So, when I have completed this, and have delivered to them what has been collected, I will set out by way of you to Spain. (Rom 15:25–28)

The way Paul mixes theology, feeling, political acumen, and practical determination can sometimes be dizzying. He laid the groundwork for his fund-raising efforts in Corinth in advance of his arrival in the city, sending a team ahead of him that consisted of Titus, an unnamed "brother whom we have often tested and found eager in many matters," and, critically, a treasurer with a reputation for independence and financial probity—"he has also been appointed by the churches to travel with us while we are administering this generous undertaking," Paul writes, adding, "We intend that no one should blame us about this generous gift that we are administering, for we intend to do what is right not only in the Lord's sight but also in the sight of others" (2 Cor 8:16–22). And even amid the anguish and self-pity that make the Second Letter to the Corinthians such an emotional document, Paul demonstrates a silky skill as a fund-raiser. He introduces the delicate subject of money by praising the Macedonian churches for their generosity: "they voluntarily gave according to their means, and even beyond their means, begging us earnestly for the privilege of sharing in this ministry to the saints [the members of the Jerusalem church]" (2 Cor 8:3–4). If this praise for another church stirred competitive instincts among the Corinthians, that was entirely intentional: "Now as you excel in everything," the flattering Paul goes on, "—in faith, in speech, in knowledge, in utmost eagerness, and in our love for you—so we want you to excel also in this generous undertaking" (2 Cor 8:7). Not, of course, that there is any pressure to cough up: "I do not say this as a command, but I am testing the genuineness of your love against the earnestness of others. For you know the generous act of our Lord Jesus Christ, that though he was rich, yet for your sakes he became poor, so that by his poverty you might become rich" (2 Cor 8:8–9).

All the same, Paul is nervous about the way his offering will be received when he reaches Jerusalem. "I appeal to you, brothers and sisters," he writes to the Romans, "by our Lord Jesus Christ and by the love of the Spirit, to join me in earnest prayer to God on my behalf, that I may be rescued from the unbelievers in Judea, and that my ministry to Jerusalem may be acceptable to the saints" (Rom 15:30–31). Those words come close to the end of the last document we have that was written by Paul himself, and their sense of foreboding is picked up by Luke in the Acts of the Apostles. The sailing season would have opened again in the spring—probably in March—but Paul's plans to leave Corinth immediately with his collection for the poor of Jerusalem ran into trouble. "He was about to set sail for Syria," Luke writes, "when a plot was made against him by the Jews, and so he decided to return through Macedonia" (Acts 20:3). Sir William Ramsay speculates that Paul was planning to make the journey on a pilgrim ship taking Jews to Jerusalem for the Passover, and that "With a shipload of hostile Jews it would be easy to find the opportunity to murder Paul."

Paul's traveling companions split up because of the plot, and when the two parties rejoin one another Luke gives us my favorite cameo moment (Acts 20:7–12). It is one of those so called "we" passages, where he seems to be drawing on a first-hand source, and it has the ring of authenticity about it; the hero has a very distinctive name (Eutychus) and it is such an odd incident that Luke can only have included it because he was convinced that it actually happened.

During a brief stopover in the port of Troas, Paul, never one to let the pace slacken, packed in some opportunistic evangelizing. After dinner with the town's Christians on the day before he was due to sail, he pounded away at his audience late into the night, evidently anxious to use every moment he could to drive his message home. The room grew hot ("There were many lamps in the room upstairs where we were meeting") and in the postprandial fog Eutychus (a "young man," according to Acts) dozed off "while Paul talked still longer." Unfortunately, Eutychus was sitting by the window; he fell three stories to the ground and "was picked up dead." Paul ran downstairs and checked him over, and then reassured the crowd "Do not be alarmed, for his life is in him."

It is important to note that Luke does not seem to be claiming that Paul actually performed a miracle—although a casual reading of the passage might lead one to think that he is. He simply reports that Paul pronounced Eutychus alive, so we must assume that the young man was not dead at all but had concussed himself in his fall. Paul is not in the least put out by this incident. Scarcely breaking stride, he goes back upstairs, grabs another bite to eat, and "continued to converse with them until dawn; then he left." Some commentators have suggested that this incident demonstrates Paul could be "less than enlivening as an orator"; I read it as rather the reverse, an indication of his capacity to hold a crowd to the end of endurance and beyond. The picture of Paul that comes through to me from Acts at this point is completely consistent with the Paul of the letters; you can imagine him pouring out ideas in an unstoppable torrent, coining new metaphors as he goes, letting that wonderfully fertile religious imagination of his play with them and reinvent them as the hours march on, stopping, finally, not because he had run out of things to say, but because daybreak called him to his ship.

It is extremely difficult for us to wind our minds back into a world where words alone could be so intoxicating; I cannot think of anyone in public life today—philosopher, preacher, scientist, or politician—who would keep an audience up for an entire night simply by talking to them. But I did get a glimpse of what a culture addicted to talk feels like while covering an entirely different story that cropped up on Paul's old bailiwick in the 1990s. Turkey has historically had very tough broadcasting restrictions, and state control of television was written into the country's constitution. But when satellite technology made it possible to broadcast into the country from abroad, an odd mixture of entrepreneurs and political activists set up pirate stations that quickly became very popular. Villages would club together to buy a satellite dish, running cables to individual homes, and before long the whole edifice of state broadcasting control collapsed under the pressure of competition. The new channels felt much freer about the subjects they covered, and issues that had previously been taboo—principally human rights abuses and the war against the Kurds—suddenly got an airing. For a while the whole country became almost

Paul of Tarsus

drunk with the thrill of free speech, and it was good ratings-chasing practice to schedule television chat shows and discussion programs that began in midevening but had no defined end time; like Paul in Troas, the guests would sometimes simply talk right through the night, and the audience went on watching, especially if the subject was a controversial one. In first-century Asia Minor, talk offered some of the best entertainment there was to be had, and having Paul in town provided the opportunity to hear a master of the art. I like to think of Eutychus desperately struggling to stay awake after a hard day's work so that he can follow Paul performing the kind of virtuoso theological improvisation he pulls off in the best of his writing.

Luke gives us another memorable set piece on the journey back to the east—Paul's farewell to his churches at the port of Miletus. It is not quite his last visit to Asia Minor (that will come when he changes ships at Myra on his way to Rome), but the Acts of the Apostles says that when he put in at Miletus he sent "a message to Ephesus, asking the elders of the church to meet him" (Acts 20:17). The speech St. Luke puts in his mouth at this point was no doubt composed with the benefit of hindsight, but bits of it have a distinctly Pauline ring to them:

> I am on my way to Jerusalem, not knowing what will happen to me there, except that the Holy Spirit testifies to me in every city that imprisonment and persecutions are waiting for me. But I do not count my life of any value to myself, if only I may finish my course and the ministry that I received from the Lord Jesus, to testify to the good news of God's grace.
> And now I know that none of you, among whom I have gone about proclaiming the kingdom, will ever see my face again. (Acts 20:22–25)

This affecting performance produced a predictable response: "There was much weeping among them all" (Acts 20:37).

9

Paul the Mythmaker

Alfred Chester Beatty had the kind of grit and dedication that make an authentic all-American plutocrat. After studying engineering at the smartest universities—Princeton and Columbia—he went to work as a laborer in the mines of the American Southwest. By the age of thirty he had made his first million, and by the time he left America for Britain in 1911 he was rich enough to indulge his passion for collecting on a really serious scale. He arrived in London as a widower, and remarried within a year, and the happy couple's choice of Egypt as a honeymoon destination was to have a profound impact on modern scholarship. Chester Beatty liked it so much that he eventually bought a house in Cairo, and during the 1920s and '30s he spent his winters there collecting Islamic and early Christian manuscripts. Ancient papyri were coming onto the market in large numbers during that period, and because they were not especially decorative they did not excite the interest of private collectors in the way they would today. The astonishing collection Chester Beatty managed to assemble, with his clear run at the best around, seemed destined for one of Britain's museums or libraries. But the great man was disgusted by the way his adopted country voted at the 1945 general election; shocked by what he saw as a betrayal of Winston Churchill and disturbed by the prospect of a socialist future, Alfred Chester Beatty moved the lot to Ireland, and the collection is now housed in the Clock Tower Building of Dublin Castle.

The earliest known edition of St. Paul's letters came into the collection almost by accident—it was discovered in a job lot of papyrus texts Chester Beatty bought in the late 1920s. It is a codex—in book form rather than a scroll—and 55 double-sided

155

pages of what would once have been a 104-page edition of Paul's work are preserved in Dublin. Each page has been sealed in glass slides to protect the papyri from the corrosive effect of the damp climate of northern Europe, and Charles Horton, the curator of Christian manuscripts at the Chester Beatty Library, let me handle a couple of slides containing pages of the First Letter to the Corinthians. The neatness of the penmanship is heroic; the ink was made from a mixture of burnt charcoal and gum arabic, and every time the scribe who wrote these documents dipped his reed pen he would have had to draw the excess ink away to avoid blotting the page—each dip would have lasted a line, or perhaps a line and a half. The individual words are not separated, so it looks like a continuous text, line upon line of Greek letters marching in impeccable step. This was a book made with dedication, love, and faith, and it would have been treasured by the church that owned it.

The Chester Beatty codex has been dated somewhere between AD 180 and 200 AD—far earlier than anything else of its kind. Sadly, its full provenance is lost forever, and we shall never know what happened to it in the seventeen-hundred years or so before it surfaced among the Cairo dealers in the early twentieth century. It may have been hidden in a period of anti-Christian Roman persecution; Eusebius records in his *Church History* that during the Diocletian persecution of AD 303 it was ordered that "the Scriptures [be] destroyed by fire," and one can readily imagine a precious book like this being hastily squirreled away somewhere, only to lie forgotten for many generations. Similarly, in the seventh century Christian monasteries throughout Egypt were burying texts in huge numbers to conceal them from the Arab armies of Islam, and many of them only came to light again when archaeology really took off in Egypt in the late nineteenth century. The pages the museum has on display have presented Charles Horton with some unusual curatorial challenges; incidents of genuflection and prayer before the exhibits are quite common, and on one occasion a group of Amish pilgrims from Pennsylvania burst into song.

There is a reason for taking this detour to Dublin while Paul makes his fateful journey along the coast of Asia Minor, carrying his collection for the poor of Jerusalem with him. If we accept the contemporary scholarly consensus about which of Paul's letters are genuine, we are now following in his footsteps without any firsthand testimony to guide us. It used to be thought that Paul's so-called prison letters were written while he was awaiting trial in Rome itself, but it is now generally accepted that they are much more likely to date from his time in Ephesus, so the Letter to the Romans was his last. From the moment Paul set sail from Corinth we must rely entirely on Luke and later church tradition for our understanding of the remaining years of his life and missionary career. So it is worth pausing for a moment or two to reflect again on the historical filters through which we see him.

What was it that made those early Christian communities decide that at least some of Paul's words were worth preserving for posterity? It is clear from the references to other correspondence in the Letters to the Corinthians that not everything Paul wrote has come down to us, and I cannot help wondering whether the recipients of some of his tougher messages were tempted to tear them up and throw them away. Albert Schweitzer was puzzled that anything of Paul's survived: "Writings like the Letter to the Galatians and the Second to the Corinthians do not really seem destined to live. How came the churches to preserve documents which redounded so little to their credit? And it is still more astonishing that they allowed their shame to be continually recalled in public worship."

Part of the answer may lie in the very straightforward fact that the arrival of any letter in the first century was a matter of some moment; the system for nonmilitary post was far too uncertain for a successful delivery to be considered routine. And because Paul seems often to have used personal envoys to carry his letters they would have arrived with some fanfare and were almost guaranteed to create a stir. Most members of the communities to which they were addressed were probably illiterate, so the letters will almost certainly have been read aloud in one of those house churches that formed the building blocks of the early Christian movement, adding to the sense of occasion that attended their reception. And we can be sure they were read and reread countless times as people puzzled over what they actually meant; the Second Letter of Peter gives us a very early piece of evidence that

Paul's letters were notorious for their complexity even in the first century—the writer admits, "There are some things in them hard to understand, which the ignorant and unstable twist to their own destruction" (2 Pet 3:16). Albert Schweitzer answers his own question like this: "How strong must have been the magic of the name of Paul, whose writings dealing with obsolete and therefore unintelligible questions and controversies, writings which contained severe strictures on contemporary churches, instead of being handed over to oblivion received the status and respect of edifying treatises." For all Paul's carping about the fickleness of his converts, his reputation clearly carried great authority in the churches he founded.

But even once we can see plausible reasons for individual communities of Pauline Christians to have kept individual letters from Paul, we face the further questions of how and by whom they came to be brought together as a single body of writing. It seems likely that they were circulating in Rome at a very early stage, because one of the first popes, Clement of Rome, alludes to them in his own Letter to the Corinthians, which is thought to have been written in AD 96. All sorts of theories have been advanced to explain how the letters were collected, and all sorts of individuals—including Timothy and Titus—have been proposed as the Chester Beatty of the first century. Archaeology is still producing surprises—like the discovery of the Dead Sea Scrolls—that open electrifyingly exciting new avenues of investigation into the past, but the answer to these questions are probably lost. There is something close to a black hole in the Christian story that lies tantalizingly between the events described in the New Testament and the emergence of something that looks more like conventional history in the second century.

We can, however, be a little more confident about the way the letters, once collected, came to be part of what we now call the biblical canon. In the earliest days of the church missionaries like Paul would have relied on oral stories about Jesus to spread their message—it seems unlikely that anything very much was written down (apart from Paul's letters, of course) and if it was it has long since been lost. The date at which the books we now know as the four gospels were composed is a source of considerable scholarly dispute, but Luke gives us an insight into the process that produced them in the preface to his own Gospel. Addressing his patron Theophilus, he writes:

> Since many have undertaken to set down an orderly account of the events that have been fulfilled among us, just as they were handed on to us by those who from the beginning were eyewitnesses and servants of the word, I too decided, after investigating everything carefully from the very first, to write an orderly account for you, most excellent Theophilus, so that you may know the truth concerning the things about which you have been instructed. (Luke 1:1–4)

Luke's reference to the "many" who had tried their hands at recording the life of Jesus suggests that there were all sorts of different versions floating around. It sounds very much as if he is writing at one remove from the primary sources, and he appears to be presenting his version of the gospel as a sort of scholarly tidying up exercise.

The Greek word *kanōn* originally meant a "reed" or "measuring stick," and thus came to represent the idea of a norm against which things could be judged. But the first person we know to have come up with a list of normative sacred texts was not a leader of the mainstream church but the heretic Marcion, who developed his ideas in the middle of the second century. Indeed it seems highly likely that the church only really felt the need to establish its own canon of authentic scripture as a response to heresy. St. Irenaeus, the bishop of Lyon, was a pivotal figure in this process, and in his book *Against Heresies* we can see the idea of a New Testament canon taking its final shape—Irenaeus includes the four gospels, the Acts of the Apostles, and St. Paul's letters. *Against Heresies* was written at roughly the time when the codex of Paul's letter in the Chester Beatty library was made, so by the end of the second century it is evident that Paul's letters were being read and used as scripture right across the Christian world from northern Africa to southern France—a very long way from the churches they were originally intended to instruct.

Irenaeus may also have played a critical role in giving the Acts of the Apostles the status Luke's book has come to enjoy. He declares that he is setting out to confound those who "have set the truth aside, and bring in lying words and vain genealogies." It is a formidable task. "Error," he says, "is never set forth in its naked deformity, lest, being thus exposed, it should at once be detected. But it is craftily decked out in an attractive dress, so as, by its outward form, to make it appear to the inexperienced...more true than the truth itself." Ireneaus's answer is to establish a corpus of sacred writing and a version of early church history that demonstrates the unity of the apostles and the consistency of Christian teaching in the earliest days of the church; this will then stand as a bulwark against heresy and a "measuring stick" against which potentially heretical ideas could be judged. The way he writes about the four gospels indicates they were already widely accepted in the Christian world—he does not seem to feel any particular need to defend their authenticity. But he is so energetic in his defence of the Acts of the Apostles that it suggests that Luke's second book was far from universally accepted.

A modern American academic, Christopher Mount, has argued that Irenaeus shoehorned the Acts into the canon because it suited his overall design. Christopher Mount believes that Acts was "either unknown or unimportant" to Irenaeus's opponents, and that the bishop of Lyons "has pulled Acts off the shelf (so to speak), dusted it off, and put it to use to establish his construction of the standard for the Gospel—a unified constellation of apostolic witnesses in scripture and tradition." Irenaeus certainly stresses the points on which Paul's letters and Acts agree (citing the Council of Jerusalem, for example) and presents Luke as a firsthand witness of the events he describes: "But that this Luke was inseparable from Paul, and his fellow laborer in the gospel, he himself evinces, not as a matter of boasting, but as bound to do so by the truth itself," he writes.

And it is to Irenaeus that we owe the identification of the Luke who wrote the Acts of the Apostles with the Luke mentioned in Paul's letters. He makes great play of the "we" passages in Acts and claims:

And Luke was present at all these occurrences, he carefully noted them down in writing, so that he cannot be convicted of falsehood, or boastfulness, because all these [particulars] proved both that he was senior to all those who now teach otherwise, and that he was not ignorant of the truth. That he was not merely a follower, but a fellow laborer of the apostles, but especially of Paul, Paul has himself declared also in the epistles, saying: "Demas has forsaken me...and is departed unto Thessalonica; Crescens to Galatia, Titus to Dalmatia. Only Luke is with me" (2 Tim 4:10, 11). And again he says, in the Epistle to the Colossians: "Luke, the beloved physician, greets you."

The two letters quoted there are, of course, now thought to have been written by someone other than Paul (although there is a reference to a Luke in the Letter to Philemon, which is genuine), and Christopher Mount argues that Irenaeus simply dreamt up this biography for the person who wrote what we now call the Gospel according to St. Luke and the Acts of the Apostles because it suited his argument. There is, he says, "no evidence that prior to Irenaeus the authorship ascription of Lk-Acts was accompanied by any traditions of the author's association with particular apostles, especially Paul." Indeed the prologue to the Gospel of Luke quoted above makes no mention of the author knowing any of the apostles or having been a witness to any of the events he describes; he writes rather of "investigating everything carefully from the first," and he would presumably not have had to do that if he had spent his time wandering around Asia Minor with St. Paul. To me, the way Luke writes about his task suggests the kind of approach you would expect today from a television documentary maker producing a film about something that happened when they were a child—say, the assassination of President Kennedy or the Cuban missile crisis. He or she would have some memory of the way the event was reported and what impact it had, but would need to conduct extensive interviews with those close to the event itself to build up a picture of what really happened.

If Christopher Mount's theory is right, then whole shelves full of scholarship—certainly including the work of men like Sir William Ramsay—are predicated on a piece of late second-century propaganda. "The supposed connection of the author of the Acts of the Apostles to Paul has," Mount argues, "caused a great deal of mischief in attempts to reconstruct Christian origins since Irenaeus." At the least it means that we have to approach the account we have of the last stages of St. Paul's career very gingerly indeed. Added to the questions about the date of the composition of the Acts and its authorship we now have a whole new set of questions about why it became a prominent element in the biblical canon.

"Luke" himself is, of course, entirely innocent of this—whoever he was and whenever he wrote, he was certainly long dead by the time Ireneaus published *Against Heresies.* A purist might argue that once we move beyond the evidence provided by the letters we do not actually "know" anything about Paul at all, but common sense suggests that is unnecessarily rigorous. The last seven chapters of Acts are absolutely packed with detail—about Paul's movements, of course, but also about areas like the imperial Roman legal system and first-century navigation, where Luke's story is susceptible to testing against independent evidence. Until this point there has only been one instance where Luke's account of Paul's life can be pinned to a date and a place by reference to evidence outside the New Testament—his appearance before the Roman official Gallio in Corinth fits with an inscription found at Delphi in 1905, which records that a certain Gallio was indeed proconsul of the region known as Achaia in the early 50s. But in this final section of Acts Paul's story repeatedly bumps into what you might call "real history"; once Paul starts to tangle with the authorities in Judea we meet all sorts of characters whose existence is recorded in secular historical accounts of this period. It is worth following Paul's footsteps to the end of the Acts of the Apostles, even though we must be extremely cautious about how we tread.

Luke builds on the sense of foreboding he introduced at Miletus, ratcheting up the tension as Paul approaches Jerusalem. When the party stops at Tyre, the Christians there warn them about going on: "Through the Spirit they told Paul not to go on to Jerusalem" (Acts 21:4). And at Caesarea a local prophet predicts that Paul will be tied up and handed over to the Roman authorities by "the Jews in Jerusalem" (Acts 21:11). But Paul insists on pressing on, and Luke gives him a remark that seems designed to prepare the way for martyrdom: "For I am ready not only to be bound but even to die in Jerusalem for the name of the Lord Jesus" (Acts 21:13).

Once Paul's party arrives in Jerusalem there is a formal meeting of the church leaders there, presided over by James: "The next day Paul went with us to visit James; and all the elders were present. After greeting them, he related one by one the things that God had done among the Gentiles through his ministry. When they heard it, they praised God" (Acts 21:18–21). It is an affecting picture—the missionary Paul describing his adventures and successes to an admiring and grateful group of his Christian "brothers" and, presumably, formally handing over his impressively substantial collection from the Gentile churches. But what happens next sounds distinctly like a frame-up. The church leaders tell Paul that there are "thousands" of Jewish followers of the Way in Jerusalem who have been scandalized by what they have heard of Paul's teaching—"They have been told about you," the church elders explain to Paul, "that you teach all the Jews living among the Gentiles to forsake Moses, and that you tell them not to circumcise their children or observe their customs" (Acts 21:21). Paul is encouraged to take part in a very Jewish ritual to demonstrate his own fidelity to the religion of his ancestors. It was considered virtuous to sponsor a pilgrim who could not afford the Temple charges and the "brothers" just happen to have four such men on hand. They suggest that Paul take on responsibility for them so that he can demonstrate to his fellow Jews "that there is nothing in what they have been told about you, but that you yourself observe and guard the law" (Acts 21:24). Paul, according to Luke's account, accepts the ruse as a politic device for dealing with the problem.

All goes well until a group of "Jews from Asia" spot Paul and recognize him as the Christian missionary who has caused so much trouble: "They seized him, shouting, 'Fellow Israelites, help! This is the man who is teaching everyone everywhere against our people, our law, and this place'" (Acts 21:27–28). On the basis of what we know of Paul from his own letters, that accusation does not seem too wide of the mark, but as Luke tells the story there is worse to come: "'more than that, he has actually brought Greeks into the temple and has defiled this holy place.' For they had previously seen Trophimus the Ephesian with him in the city, and they supposed that Paul had brought him into the temple" (Acts 21:28–29).

There are all sorts of things about this account that do not quite add up. The original proposal that Paul use this device to prove himself in the eyes of Jewish followers of the Way comes from the leaders of the Jerusalem church, and that begs an obvious question: why on earth could they not use their authority to state their support for Paul openly? He had after all come to Jerusalem of his own volition, bringing a significant financial contribution. James's position as a "pillar" of the church is recognized in both Acts and Paul's own letters, so it seems reasonable to assume that other believers would have taken what he had to say seriously. Even if we accept that the plan was put to Paul in good faith it seems to contain a flaw: its success depended on Paul making a public demonstration of his adherence to Jewish tradition, but as soon as he is publicly identified he runs into trouble. Finally, if the Jews from Asia had already spotted Paul out and about in Jerusalem with his Ephesian friend Trophimus and allowed him to go about his business unmolested, what was it that suddenly made them decide that he had polluted the Temple?

There is a very cynical interpretation of this incident that, if true, sheds an extremely unflattering light on the early church— that a group of Paul's rivals deliberately set him up by proposing a scheme they knew would get him into trouble, and that they closed the trap on him by putting it about that he was guilty of Temple pollution. There is a hint that the story was told that way in the early church in the Letter to the Corinthians from Pope Clement; he says that it was through "jealousy and envy" that Paul was persecuted and killed. Certainly what followed when Paul was set upon in the Temple was rather more than the usual Pauline ruckus; indeed Luke's account suggests that this was altogether more serious than anything Paul had endured to date. The riot was noisy enough to bring the troops of the Roman garrison out of their barracks, and Luke makes it clear they only just arrived in time to prevent Paul from being beaten to death. The Roman officer in charge of security in Jerusalem decided to take him into protective custody, and when the troops got him to the steps of the Antonia fortress "the violence of the mob was so great that he had to be carried by the soldiers" (Acts 21:35).

There is no evidence of James or any of the other "brothers" who welcomed Paul so warmly to Jerusalem only a few days earlier coming to his assistance or even going to visit him in jail. At this point the Jerusalem church disappears from the narrative of the Acts of the Apostles altogether. Everything about this stage of Paul's life is of course known only in the most tentative way, but the little evidence we have suggests the following facts. He had, as he told the Christians of Rome, come to Jerusalem desperately hoping that the money given by his Gentile churches would provide a means to build bridges with their Jewish co-religionists. He had spent the previous months developing a theology of salvation that allowed for the eventual redemption of the Jewish people, and made his own mission a pivotal factor in that process; out of that vision he had crafted a masterpiece, the Letter to the Romans, which still stands as one of the towering achievements of religious creativity. Yet he had been completely abandoned—perhaps even deliberately betrayed—by the Christians of Jerusalem. We know from his letters how keenly he felt disloyalty when it was the work of those he had believed to be close to him, and one can only imagine his emotions as he sat in his cell in the Antonia fortress next door to the Temple.

The only help he gets comes from that mysterious nephew who pops up out of nowhere to warn Paul that his enemies are planning to lure him out of Roman protection so that they can do him in:

> In the morning the Jews joined in a conspiracy and bound themselves by an oath neither to eat nor drink until they had killed Paul. There were more than forty who joined in this conspiracy. They went to the chief priests and elders and said, "We have strictly bound

ourselves by an oath to taste no food until we have killed Paul. Now then, you and the council must notify the tribune to bring him down to you, on the pretext that you want to make a more thorough examination of his case. And we are ready to do away with him before he arrives." (Acts 23:12–15)

When news of this conspiracy is brought to the attention of the tribune, Claudius Lysias, he arranges for Paul to be spirited away under cover of darkness, with the protection of "two hundred soldiers, seventy horsemen, and two hundred spearmen" (Acts 23:23).

If that seems an excessively large escort for a figure who can scarcely have been well known in Jerusalem (it was many years since Paul had been anything like a permanent resident of the city), it is perhaps explained by the context in which the Roman commander took his decision. A report of an assassination plot would have seemed entirely plausible to Claudius Lysias, because the Sicarii had become a serious menace by this stage: "They made use of small swords," Josephus records, "not much different in length from the Persian *acinacae,* but somewhat crooked, and like the Roman *sicae* (or sickles) as they were called; and from those weapons these robbers got their denomination; and with these weapons they slew a great many." In AD 54 the Sicarii had killed the High Priest Jonathon (presumably for collaborating with the Romans, although it has also been suggested that he was the victim of a sinister conspiracy between the terrorists and the Roman authorities). The hit was carried out in the style for which they were famous—they mixed with the crowd to get close to him with their daggers concealed beneath their coats—and Josephus reports that they went on something of a killing spree: "The robbers went up with the greatest security at the festivals at this time and having weapons concealed in like manner as before, and mingling themselves with the multitude, they slew certain of their own enemies." They even had the brazenness to murder people in the Temple itself "without thinking of the impiety of which they were guilty," and rallied crowds of supporters outside the city walls of Jerusalem with the promise of "manifest wonders and signs."

Paul the Mythmaker

The Roman governor, Marcus Antonius Felix, had to spend a good deal of this energies dealing with these disturbances. There was an especially troublesome "prophet" from Egypt who stirred up more trouble in the countryside and claimed he could bring down the walls of Jerusalem simply by ordering them to fall. Felix sent out a mixed contingent of cavalry and infantry who killed four hundred of the Egyptian's supporters and captured another two hundred, but—like some first-century Osama bin Laden—the ringleader himself gave them the slip, and the Romans were extremely keen to track him down. Indeed when the Jerusalem garrison commander Claudius Lysias first took Paul into custody, he asked him whether he was "the Egyptian who recently stirred up a revolt and led the four thousand assassins out into the wilderness" (Acts 21:38). The Roman authorities were understandably jittery—against this background of bubbling political violence they were not going to take any chances with Paul.

Sir William Ramsay has pointed out, "From the moment when Paul was arrested onwards, the narrative becomes much fuller," and he suggests that this reflects a general principle that holds good throughout the Acts—that "Luke devotes special attention...to the occasions on which Paul was brought in contact with Roman officials." We saw in the last chapter that his encounters with Roman officialdom are usually benign, and that tendency becomes even more marked now, even though Paul is a Roman prisoner by this stage. The contrast with the extremely unsatisfactory ending of his contact with the Jerusalem church is striking. The description of Paul's imprisonment at this point adds weight to the theory that Acts was designed to produce a reassuring body of evidence that Roman imperial power and Christianity are natural allies, not enemies.

At the port of Caesarea—another architectural triumph left behind by Herod the Great with his mania for monumental building—Paul's escort deliver him into the custody of the Roman procurator himself. Marcus Antonius Felix was very much a "real" historical figure, and features in the works of Josephus, Suetonius, and Tacitus. He was the first ever "freed man" to rise to the rank of procurator—he began life as a slave in the household of Mark Antony's daughter Antonia—and he enjoyed the good fortune his name suggests. His brother was one of Claudius's favorites—which cannot have hurt his rise to power—and he had a remarkable knack for marrying princesses; his second wife was the granddaughter of Antony and Cleopatra, and by the time he met Paul he was on his third, Drusilla, who was the daughter of King Herod Agrippa I. Tacitus described him in characteristically epigrammatic style as a man who "exercised the prerogative of a king, with all the cruelty and lust in the spirit of a slave." However, the way he appears in the Acts of the Apostles suggests he was savvy and venal, but not especially cruel.

He summons the High Priest down to Caesarea to make the case against Paul, and Ananias appears with a smart lawyer called Tertullus. Tertullus accuses Paul in terms he clearly believes are guaranteed to set the Roman authorities against him: "We have, in fact," he declares, "found this man a pestilent fellow, an agitator among all the Jews throughout the world, and a ringleader of the sect of the Nazarenes" (Acts 24:5). But St. Luke says that Felix "was rather well informed about the Way" and was not entirely convinced by the case Tertullus made. He decided to put off making a decision on Paul's case and placed him under house arrest. This state of affairs apparently lasted for two years, during which Felix evidently thought that the matter might be resolved by a bribe: "he hoped that money would be given him by Paul, and for that reason he used to send for him very often and converse with him" (Acts 24:26). No doubt the occasional opportunity to preach at a Roman procurator was diverting for Paul, but he must have become fantastically frustrated; on past form two years would certainly have been enough time for him to fulfill his ambition to open up a whole new missionary field in Spain. In a famous poem on Paul's imprisonment, Cardinal Newman wonders whether he was kept going by his confidence in the divine plan that dictated that he should spend some time "loitering for Jesu's sake."

Things come to a head when Felix is replaced by a new procurator, Porcus Festus. Festus pays an early visit to Jerusalem and finds the "chief priests and the leaders of the Jews" as determined as ever to pursue their case against Paul. Seeking to exploit the natural anxiety of a new governor to ingratiate himself with his subjects, they ask that Paul be brought back to Jerusalem for trial. Luke is convinced this is a ruse to allow them to revive the plot against Paul that was frustrated when he was taken into Roman custody: "They were, in fact," he writes, "planning an ambush to kill him along the way" (Acts 25:3). Festus anyway refuses their request, but he does agree to reopen the case against Paul, and it is now that the apostle famously exercises his full rights as a Roman citizen by appealing to the emperor in Rome. "Festus, after he had conferred with his council, replied, 'You have appealed to the emperor; to the emperor you will go'" (Acts 25:12). There is some question about Luke's interpretation of Roman law at this point, because he has Paul making this appeal of the last resort before he has actually been convicted of anything. But there is no doubt about the way Luke regards the symbolic significance of Paul's statement; for him this is the moment when the Apostle to the Gentiles finally and decisively turns his back on his Jewish past and signs up to the rules of the Roman Empire where Christianity will put down its enduring roots.

Before dispatching Paul to Rome, Luke gives him one more set-piece opportunity to rehearse his *apologia*. His case is heard all over again when Festus receives a formal visit from King Herod Agrippa II and his sister Bernice. These two were among the most colorful of all the characters the apostle encountered. Herod Agrippa was the great-grandson of Herod the Great. He had been born in Rome and ruled as a puppet of the Romans. However, his responsibilities included the selection of the High Priest in the Temple at Jerusalem, so he was a figure of some consequence in Judaism. Berenice (as she is better known) was an extraordinary figure. She had been married three times by this stage—her second husband was her uncle, Herod, king of Chalcis, by whom she had two sons—and her relationship with Herod Agrippa was widely thought to be incestuous. She later seduced the emperor Titus and in her forties became his established mistress despite being his senior by a decade, and her story was immortalized by Racine in an eponymous tragedy. The couple would undoubtedly have featured regularly in a first-century version of *People* magazine. Paul was apparently unfazed by their celebrity and gave a cool and convincing account of himself, going through his Road to Damascus routine all over again.

The hearing ends with an odd piece of dialogue. After listening to Paul's speech, the king declares him to be innocent but says that he must go to Rome nonetheless: "Then the king got up, and with him the governor and Bernice and those who had been seated with them; and as they were leaving, they said to one another, 'This man is doing nothing to deserve death or imprisonment.' Agrippa said to Festus, 'This man could have been set free if he had not appealed to the emperor'" (Acts 26:30–32). Why on earth should an appeal to the emperor mean that Paul *had* to be sent to Rome, despite being judged innocent? It simply does not make sense. Luke seems to have lost his grip on his material at this point, and one can only conclude that this confusing little exchange was inserted to reconcile two apparently irreconcilable narrative imperatives: Paul had to be found innocent to help make Luke's point about the apostle's harmonious relationship with the Roman authorities, but he also had to be taken to Rome as a prisoner for the story to work.

The account of Paul's sea voyage to Rome is largely devoid of anything you might describe as theology, but it is a ripping adventure story. Nelson is said to have read the twenty-seventh chapter of Acts on the morning of the battle of Copenhagen, and for Victorian enthusiasts the vivid narrative and the wealth of nautical detail offered proof positive that Luke was a serious historian. The energy of one Victorian scientist, James Smith, a Fellow of the Royal Society no less, can stand for that of the many who followed Paul round the Mediterranean. He records that he stayed for a whole winter on Malta, visiting the bay where Paul is believed to have been shipwrecked in the appropriate weather conditions, crossexamining ships' captains and pilots about seafaring in the Mediterranean, and studying the maps and manuscripts preserved in the library of the Knights of Malta. The next summer was spent in the libraries and museums of Naples, Florence, Lausanne, and Paris, and he finally returned to London to complete his research by rummaging around in the medals room of the British Museum and reading Admiralty records of early court-martials in the Royal Navy. The result is infectiously obsessive; pages of calculations designed to establish the likely tonnage of the ship that carried Paul on his way to Rome, elaborate experiments to demonstrate the arrangement of its oars, and careful study of the prevailing winds in the eastern Mediterranean—all designed to demonstrate Luke's extraordinary grasp of the technical aspects of first-century seamanship. Modern scholars—spoilsports that they can sometimes be—are more likely to focus on the textual inconsistencies that suggest that Luke was drawing on several different sources that did not always agree at this point. There are significant differences between some of the early biblical texts in the way this section of Acts is reproduced, and it is sometimes suggested that Luke has conflated the accounts of two separate journeys to Rome.

The climax of the story is the shipwreck in Malta. Paul's ship is driven for days before a storm, a crisis that allows him to demonstrate what one can only describe as "officer quality"; he gives the crew pep talks to keep their spirits up and insists that they eat to maintain their strength. Eventually they sight land, and Luke's account of what happens next demonstrates that he can be a fine storyteller, whatever his failures as a historian:

> In the morning they did not recognize the land, but they noticed a bay with a beach, on which they planned to run the ship ashore, if they could. So they cast off the anchors and left them in the sea. At the same time they loosened the ropes that tied the steering-oars; then hoisting the foresail to the wind, they made for the beach. But striking a reef, they ran the ship aground; the bow stuck and remained immovable, but the stern was being broken up by the force of the waves. The soldiers' plan was to kill the prisoners, so that none might swim away and escape; but the centurion, wishing to save Paul, kept them from carrying out their plan. He ordered those who could swim to jump overboard first and make for the land, and the rest to follow, some on planks and others on pieces of the ship. And so it was that all were brought safely to land. (Acts 27:39–44)

H. V. Morton judged this chapter to be "the finest piece of writing in Acts," and declares that Luke's "account of the manoeuvrings of the ship, and of its wreck on Malta, are the most vivid descriptions of such happenings in ancient literature." The picture Luke draws of the moments after the ship ran aground on a sandbank is certainly dramatic, and he gives us just enough to imagine the intensity of the emotions as, with the waves breaking around them, the soldiers drew their swords and turned on Paul and his fellow prisoners, only to be held back at the last moment by a shout from their officer.

This account is believed with unshakeable conviction on the island of Malta today, and the cult of Paul is absolutely central to the way modern Maltese Catholicism understands itself. According to Acts, Paul converted the "leading man" of the island, one Publius, by curing his father. Maltese tradition takes on the story by making Publius the first bishop of Malta, and holds that the cathedral that now stands in the old capital, Mdina, is built on the site of Publius's house, a permanent reminder of the apostolic origins of the island's faith. And shortly after his arrival Paul performed a modest miracle that gave birth to an engaging Pauline myth. The Maltese lit a fire so that Paul and his companions could dry off, and "Paul had gathered a bundle of brushwood and was putting it on the fire, when a viper, driven out by the heat, fastened itself on his hand" (Acts 28:3). Instead of swelling up and dropping down dead as everyone expects, Paul insouciantly "shook off the creature into the fire and suffered no harm" (Acts 28:5). The Maltese insist that poisonous snakes have been banished from the island ever since—a somewhat unflattering version of this legend holds that Paul removed the poison from the viper's fangs and put it into the tongues of the Maltese instead.

There is an ancient challenge to Malta's claim to be the site of Paul's shipwreck. There were two islands called "Melita" by the Romans, and the second is now known as Melida and lies just off the Dalmatian coast. Its partisans point to Luke's description of Paul's ship "drifting across the sea of Adria [the Adriatic]" just before it makes land (Acts 27:27), and the Benedictine monks who settled on Melida in the sixteenth century campaigned enthusiastically for their island's place in the Paul story. No one gives the claim much credence today, but this heated competition for an association with Paul underlines the fact that at this point in the Acts of the Apostles he is on the point of slipping into the world of myth, folk memory, and church tradition. At the end of chapter 28 of St. Luke's work he disappears altogether from the New Testament.

The end of Acts is one of the world's great literary mysteries. From Malta Luke moves Paul briskly on to Rome and settles him there. He was under house arrest but apparently allowed to enjoy a considerable degree of freedom, because he soon began holding characteristically extended seminars on the Christian faith ("they came to him at his lodgings in great numbers," St. Luke relates. "From morning until evening he explained the matter to them," Acts 28:23). We are told that Paul had mixed success with Rome's Jews, and he is given a valedictory speech to ram home the message that he has turned his back on Judaism and embraced the Roman world. Quoting Isaiah's description of the way the Jews have rejected God ("For this people's heart has grown dull, and their ears are hard of hearing, and they have shut their eyes..." Acts 28:27), Paul concludes: "Let it be known to you then that this salvation of God has been sent to the Gentiles; they will listen" (Acts 28:28). And then we get this: "He lived there [in Rome] for two whole years at his own expense and welcomed all who came to him, proclaiming the kingdom of God and teaching about the Lord Jesus Christ with all boldness and without hindrance" (Acts 28:30–31).

And that is it—*point finale*. There is no trial before the emperor, no account of a prolonged imprisonment, no praise for another sally into successful proselytizing, no reunion with St. Peter, no description of a glorious martyrdom. This towering New Testament figure—who only a chapter ago was standing before us as such a commanding and lifelike figure amid the foaming seas of a Maltese bay—simply drops out of sight.

All sorts of explanations have been offered for the conundrum that St. Luke has left us. Some of those who persist in believing that Luke was one of Paul's companions suggest that Acts was written to serve as the case for the defense at the apostle's trial, and that Luke did not finish the story because it was not over. There are two problems with this theory. The first is that the end of Acts is clearly written in a way that encourages the reader to expect some kind of confrontation with the emperor (during that storm on Paul's journey to Rome, for example, an angel appears and tells him, "Do not be afraid, Paul; you must stand before the emperor," Acts 27:24). The second is elegantly put by A. N. Wilson:

> If you believe that Acts was written down before Paul's trial (the idea proposed is that it is in a sense a brief being offered to some senior Roman official before the trial to make him think the best of the defendant) then you have to accept the strange fact that no one—after the trial was over—ever thought to append a note to the end of Acts saying, "and by the way, he got off"; or "in spite of our best endeavours, the case went against brother Paul and he had his head chopped off."

Then there is the ingenious suggestion that Luke knew the outcome of Paul's trial but chose to keep quiet about it because he felt it would damage the objective of his book; if he was writing to demonstrate to the Roman world that it could live harmoniously with Christianity, then it might be unhelpful to describe a trial that ended with one of the central figures of the new religion being put to death. But one cannot help thinking that Luke's audience would have found his reticence somewhat suspicious.

There are also a couple of more theological reasons put forward for Luke taking a deliberate decision to keep silent about Paul's fate. An account of Paul's death might have been read as too close a parallel to Christ's passion, and Luke wanted to avoid all doubt that a focus on Jesus, not Paul, was the proper foundation for Christian faith. Equally if he saw Acts as first and foremost an account of the way the gospel was spread—rather than the biography of a remarkable man—he may have felt that Paul's arrival in Rome to proclaim the good news was indeed the climax of the story he was trying to tell; what happened to Paul afterward becomes irrelevant according to this theory, and to set it down would entail the risk of making him, rather than the gospel, the true hero of Acts.

It is just possible that Luke was simply ignorant about Paul's fate, but that seems extremely unlikely. The obvious answer to the problem is that he wrote another book that has been lost, and the obvious answer is often the right one. But this mystery must in the end join the many others on the list of Pauline puzzles that will never be solved. A. N. Wilson enjoys telling the story of Oscar Wilde's *viva voce* exam at Oxford. Wilde was set a passage of Greek to translate that is considered the most difficult in the New Testament—that twenty-seventh chapter of Acts with all its technical nautical terms. After a few minutes of effortless oral translation the examiners had heard enough and asked him to stop, but Oscar Wilde would have nothing of it. "Oh please!" he replied. "Do let me go on—I am longing to know how the story finishes." "Like many of Wilde's jokes," A. N. Wilson observes, "it contains a great profundity." Paul has had such a powerful impact on Western civilization that his story still is not really over today.

10

Our Paul

On November 21, 1964, Pope Paul VI solemnly promulgated *Lumen gentium,* a new "Dogmatic Constitution on the Church." It was a centerpiece of the Second Vatican Council, the Catholic Church's attempt to open itself up to the modern world, and it begins in unashamedly grand style:

> Christ is the Light of nations. Because this is so, this Sacred Synod gathered together in the Holy Spirit eagerly desires, by proclaiming the Gospel to every creature, to bring the light of Christ to all men, a light brightly visible on the countenance of the Church. Since the Church is in Christ like a sacrament or as a sign and instrument both of a very closely knit union with God and of the unity of the whole human race, it desires now to unfold more fully to the faithful of the Church and to the whole world its own inner nature and universal mission.

Lumen gentium is a wonderful document, generous-spirited and very "Pauline" in its overall tone. It stresses the universality of the Christian message—its chapter "On the People of God" begins, "At all times and in every race God has given welcome to whosoever fears Him and does what is right"—and it consigned to history the traditional Catholic exclusivity expressed in the old saw, *"nulla salus extra ecclesiam"* (there is no salvation outside the church). Together with its companion document *Gaudium et spes* (on the church in the modern world), *Lumen gentium* provided the intellectual foundation for the great explosion of Catholic energy and thinking that Vatican II ignited in the developing world.

The Catholic Church cannot of course simply make things up as it goes along, even when it is meeting in one of those councils of the world's bishops that are designed to settle great questions of doctrine. Everything it says must have a foundation in scripture and tradition, so *Lumen gentium,* like all the council documents, is accompanied by a formidable apparatus of footnotes that is designed to supply a biblical basis for its conclusions. The 304 scriptural references appended to the document include no less than 167 allusions to the 13 Pauline letters of the New Testament canon. In both spirit and the sheer statistical weight of quotable quotes quoted, this seminal twentieth-century document is, one might argue, Paul's work; nearly two millennia and more than twenty councils after the first Council of Jerusalem at which he squared up to Peter, Paul's influence was still a dominant intellectual force. Different parts of Paul's message have appealed to different generations of Christians; the Second Vatican Council was the apotheosis of what we would now call the "inclusivity" of his vision.

And yet there are things about *Lumen gentium* that Paul would have regarded with bewilderment, and perhaps horror too. The very idea of a church constitution would have been entirely alien to him. What on earth would the great iconoclast and enemy of religion as rules have made of a chapter devoted to "The Hierarchical Structure of the Church and in Particular the Episcopate"? The continued existence of a church so organized and mighty that it could call more than two thousand bishops together to sit in their finery within the extravagant splendor of St. Peter's would have shaken him to the core. Paul preached the imminence of the Second Coming, yet the church he helped to found has become the most enduring institution in history; the Vatican is the most emphatic rebuttal of the idea of imminent *parousia* it is possible to imagine.

Paul thrived on argument and debate, and challenged the intellectual status quo almost as a matter of reflex; the Catholic Church has often in its history been regarded as a byword for intellectual rigidity and authoritarianism. And while Paul's whole idea of religion is posited on his rejection of a set of regulations as the path to salvation, even as "liberal" a document as *Lumen gentium* reasserts the church's "infallibility" in "defining doctrine of faith and morals"; Paul preached against enslavement to the Law, but his church went on to invent a whole new "Law" of its own.

As soon as you contemplate Paul's writings and his life in relation to his legacy, the paradoxes pile up. It is especially striking in Rome, because the city is so full of reminders of the tension between Paul and Peter, and the Pauline and Petrine strands in Christianity. They would presumably have been there together if the Christian tradition is accurate, and it is impossible not to wonder how they got on with one another after the rows of Antioch and Jerusalem. The earliest account we have of a joint mission comes at several removes in both time and place. Writing in the early fourth century, Eusebius, the bishop of Caesarea, quotes a second-century letter to the Romans from one Dionysius, bishop of Corinth: "You have bound together all that has grown from the seed that Peter and Paul have sowed in Romans and Corinthians alike. For both of them sowed in our Corinth, and taught us jointly; in Italy too they taught jointly in the same city, and were martyred at the same time." We can be as sure as it is possible to be at this distance that Peter and Paul never worked together in Corinth (Paul would certainly have mentioned it in his letters) so this does not provide exactly compelling evidence that they joined forces in Rome. But the city is soaked in the tradition that both these great apostles are buried there after being martyred at roughly the same date.

Paul should surely have been more comfortable in Rome than Peter. He was, after all, a Diaspora Jew who grew up with a strong sense of Hellenistic culture, and spent many years moving easily between the great cities of the empire. He was a Roman citizen who had, by St. Luke's account, become thoroughly accustomed to dealing with the Roman authorities. And as he tells us in the Letter to the Galatians, he, not Peter, was the Apostle to the Gentiles; "I had been entrusted with the gospel for the uncircumcised," he informs them, "just as Peter had been trusted with the gospel for the circumcised" (Gal 2:7). And yet it is the fisherman from Galilee, not Paul, who becomes the first bishop of

Rome. If you visit the Eternal City with the idea of a rivalry between Peter and Paul in mind, you find Peter's victory written everywhere in its stones.

I had not fully appreciated the hold St. Peter has on the soul of Rome until I went deep beneath the Vatican to visit the *scavi*. These excavations began with one of those chance discoveries that make archaeology such an enticing adventure. In 1939 a group of workmen digging out a grave for Pope Pius XI in the crypt of St. Peter's uncovered what was plainly the top of a Roman building. The new Pope, Pius XII, ordered further investigation, and archaeologists uncovered a well-preserved Roman necropolis—or city of the dead—immediately below the foundations of St. Peter's. They opened it up and secured it. With an eerie awareness of the tourists admiring Michelangelo's dome above your head, you can now walk down subterranean streets lined with frescoed mausoleums. And at the heart of this complex the Vatican's archaeologists discovered what they believed to be the tomb of St. Peter.

It took them a couple of years to find the bones that belonged to it—the fresh-faced American seminarian leading my group on our subterranean pilgrimage told a charming story about an absentminded monsignor who wandered off with the bundle without realizing what it was—and many more years of tests to establish their secrets. They were found, for example, to have been stained with purple dye, which meant they had at some stage been wrapped up in an expensive cloth. In 1976 Pope Paul VI felt confident enough to declare that St. Peter's remains had been discovered. They are now preserved in an acrylic plastic box designed by the American space agency NASA, and Pope John Paul II asked for them to be brought to his hospital bedroom when he was recovering from the assassination attempt against him in 1981.

For the church, what really mattered about this discovery was that it proved that the heart of Roman Catholicism beats in the right place: "If you were to hang a plumb line from the very tip of the cupola [of St. Peter's] 460 feet up," our pious guide explained, "it would go through the sixteenth-century altar [which you see in the center of St. Peter's today], then through the twelfth-century altar of Callistus, through the sixth-century altar of Gregory the Great, then through the fourth-century Constantine shrine, down to the second-century trophy [a kind of triumphal arch built to mark the burial place of great men] and would land on the grave of this martyr of Christ, St. Peter. It doesn't miss a foot. It is almost as though you can see that verse written in stone: 'Upon this rock I shall build my church.'" From the very earliest days, St. Peter's place at the center of the church—figuratively and literally—has been fixed.

St. Paul's spirit, by contrast, walks a good distance from the busy streets around the Vatican. His bones are said to lie at the Church of St. Paul's Outside the Walls, which, as its name suggests, is well beyond the boundaries of ancient Rome. It is one of my favorite Roman churches, partly because it takes you so much by surprise—there is something almost suburban about its setting, yet it is almost as grand and monumental as St. Peter's itself. There is a Benedictine monastery attached to the basilica, and when I talked to the abbot, Dom Paolo, he spoke with an odd mixture of humility and pride about Paul's place in the life of both Rome and the church. "His letters and theology are very difficult," he said apologetically, "and his tomb was fairly hidden here even though the basilica is large.... It was out of the way, off the beaten track." Even the monks who settled here in the eighth century, he explained, only spent the winter months at the monastery because it was built on marshland, and became a fever pit during the summer. But Dom Paolo took somewhat wistful comfort from a recent archaeological discovery. "A few years ago," he told me in the monastic parlor, "they found a small boat, a symbol of the church, in the catacombs. St. Peter was at the helm, but St. Paul stood at the prow, pointing ahead. That is interesting."

Father Scott Brodeur, the Jesuit theologian I so unkindly challenged as we stood between the statues of Peter and Paul in the piazza of the Vatican, sees the tension between the two great saints as the dialectic driving Christian history: "Peter and his descendants, the popes, stand for centralized church authority represented by Rome," he said, "and Paul, this great missionary, for the truth of the gospel, the freedom of the gospel, and how that was interpreted by the Protestants during the Reformation." It was, he said, "a healthy tension"; he admitted his heart was with St. Paul, even though he had, as a Catholic priest, declared his allegiance to the pope.

The way the two men were remembered by the church tells us something about the way the early Christians came to think about their new faith. Peter could offer something that Paul could not—direct contact with the living Jesus; that made him a guarantor of the legitimacy of the Christian church in a way that Paul could never be. It has become increasingly fashionable to pose the question, "Was Paul rather than Jesus the true founder of Christianity?" Perhaps the early Christians had a sense of it too, and placing Peter at the center of their Roman stage was a way of insisting on Jesus' preeminence. It is a question asked by both Paul's enemies and his friends, and it has been pushing itself insistently to the front of my mind throughout the writing of this book.

Anyone who reads St. Paul's letters cannot fail to be struck by how seldom he quotes the teaching of Jesus directly, and how little he has to say about his life before his passion. Certainly there are allusions to statements that were made, according to the gospels, by Jesus himself; thus Paul declares in the love hymn of the First Letter to the Corinthians that "if I have all faith, so as to remove mountains, but do not have love, I am nothing" (1 Cor 13:2), which seems a clear echo of Jesus' teaching that "if you have faith the size of a mustard seed, you will say to this mountain, 'Move from here to there,' and it will move" (Matt 17:20). And it is reasonable to argue, as James Dunn of Durham University did when I put this conundrum to him, that Paul was writing to communities whom he had already taught about Jesus. Since the basic facts about Jesus' teaching had been passed on by Paul during his initial evangelization, Professor Dunn said, he "didn't need to reteach it."

But you might still expect Paul to use the odd phrases like "as Jesus said," or to repeat the occasional parable when he wants to drive a point home—he is, after all, a prolific quoter of what we now call Old Testament biblical sources. But he does nothing of the kind. The voice of the Paul we hear across the centuries is not that of a disciple who is trying to disseminate his Master's message in the straightforward manner of a teacher; it is that of a prophet who has been granted a unique—and divinely inspired—

understanding of what that message was. Paul's letters are not about what Jesus did and said, they are about what his life, and, critically, his death and resurrection, really meant.

Our tendency to confuse the chronology of the New Testament's composition is perhaps inevitable. Because Jesus lived before Paul went on his missionary wanderings, it is natural for us to read the gospels as if they were written before his letters. But since, as we have seen, it is in fact almost certain that the letters were written before anything else, we are bound to distort the way we absorb the New Testament. Twenty years may have elapsed between the moment when Paul dictated the words that open his first Letter to the Thessalonians—"I, Paul, Silvanus, and Timothy, To the church of the Thessalonians in God the Father and the Lord Jesus Christ; Grace to you and peace" (1 Thess 1:1)—and the moment when the author of the Gospel of Mark began collecting the stories about Jesus' life in what many have argued is the oldest of the four canonical gospels. That means, for example, that verses 23 to 26 of the eleventh chapter of the First Letter to the Corinthians give us by far the oldest description we have of the origins of the Eucharist, even though most of us are probably more familiar with the story as it appears in the gospels. We cannot know whether Paul's account is more accurate simply because it is older, and we equally cannot know if the gospel authors had read Paul's letters—indeed Luke's failure to mention the letters in the Acts of the Apostles suggests that he, at least, had not. But we can be reasonably sure that the four evangelists were writing in a Christian context that had been at least partly shaped by his influence.

The task of identifying the distinctively "Pauline" elements of the religion that has formed so much of Western civilization is further complicated by the way huge theological edifices have been built on what he wrote. Some of the great theological doctrines—and indeed disputes—of Christianity can be traced back to odd paragraphs or even phrases in St. Paul's letters. Almost in passing, for example, he tells the Corinthians that they have been "bought with a price" (1 Cor 6:20)—it is a vivid way of bringing home the idea that a Christian belongs to Christ as a slave belongs to his master. Over time the phrase got caught up with the classical doctrine of atonement, and theologians began to ask rather more of the metaphor than St. Paul is likely to have intended. As the *Catholic Encyclopaedia* puts it, "When a captive is ransomed the price is naturally paid to the conqueror by whom he is held in bondage. Hence, if this figure were taken and interpreted literally in all its details, it would seem that the price of man's ransom must be paid to Satan. This notion is certainly startling, if not revolting." Arguments over the question of whether the doctrine of the atonement implies the devil has some kind of original ownership over humankind caused discord and mischief among Christians for at least a millennium.

To take another example, later in the same letter St. Paul instructs the Corinthians to reflect on the state of their consciences before taking communion: "Whoever, therefore, eats the bread or drinks the cup of the Lord in an unworthy manner will be answerable for the body and blood of the Lord. Examine yourselves, and only then eat of the bread and drink of the cup. For all who eat and drink without discerning the body, eat and drink judgment against themselves" (1 Cor 11:27–29). St. Paul clearly intended that the Corinthians should take the sacrament of the Eucharist seriously; whether he meant to terrify future generations of Christians with the terrible threat that communion taken in a state of sin would mean automatic damnation—which is the way this text came to be interpreted, especially in the Protestant churches—is an altogether different matter.

Paul's style must be held partly responsible for the development of a Christian reflex of turning almost everything he said into an instant dogma. Standing on their own, passages like those I have quoted above have a lapidary quality and a finality about them that make them sound like declarations of eternal truth. It is difficult to say exactly when the belief that Paul's words needed to be treated with the full reverence due to the word of God became settled. One of the church's earliest theologians, Origen, accepts that Paul sometimes makes judgments that are purely personal, and points to the distinction Paul himself makes between his teaching and that of Jesus on the matter of divorce (1 Cor 7:12). But by the time St. John Chrysostom, the bishop of Constantinople, was delivering his homilies on St. Paul's epistles in the last years of the fourth century, it was evidently orthodox to accept everything that Paul wrote as if Christ were speaking through him.

But taking Paul's quotable quotes out of their context is a little like another bad literary habit—extracting a nicely turned couplet from a Shakespeare soliloquy and presenting it as a moral principle. That is not to suggest that Paul's letters are fiction, but it is to recognize that they have a dramatic and dynamic quality about them. Can we really hold him fully responsible for all the elaborate and sometimes tottering theological structures that were built over the centuries on the foundation of his letters? Much of it would have been as bewildering to him as it would have been to the Jesus of Galilee.

The only really sensible way to approach the question of whether Paul was the true founder of Christianity is to accept that we have to be content with extremely tentative answers. At a minimum we should recognize that it was Paul who made it possible for Christianity to become a world religion. We must assume that Jesus remained an observant Jew throughout his life; otherwise it makes no sense that those who had known him well—like James and Peter—should have continued to observe the Law long after his death, plainly regarding it as an essential precondition to salvation until Paul challenged them from Antioch. Evidently Jesus' teaching had a sufficiently powerful appeal to draw followers across the Roman Empire without Paul's help, because we know that the Way became established in Rome before his visit there, and, indeed, in that other great metropolis Alexandria, which he never visited at all. But Paul's determination that the gospel should offer salvation to all humanity must surely have been the catalyst that made it possible for this new religion to put down roots outside the Jewish community and to establish itself eventually as part of the fabric of the Roman Empire.

We must also acknowledge the creativity of the way Paul developed the idea of crucifixion. There are those who argue that because he gave such a central place to Christ's passion the gospels simply followed his lead: "The Shadow of the Cross," A. N. Wilson writes, "and its Glory (to use a very Pauline word), dominate and animate the pages of all four Gospels, revealing them to belong to the world which Paul has imaginatively transformed." The idea that Paul is responsible for the way the crucifixion is treated by the gospel writers makes assumptions about the composition of the gospels that I do not feel qualified to judge, but there is no doubt that Paul manages to transform the crucifixion into a uniquely powerful metaphor (and by using that word I do no mean in any way to cast doubt on the reality of Christ on the cross). I asked Wayne Meeks, one of the most thorough of contemporary Paul scholars, to sum up what Paul gave to Christianity: "a habit of reading the story of the crucifixion and the resurrection of Christ as a root metaphor which could be used as a pattern for the whole form of life of Christianity." That does not make Paul the founder of Christianity, but it does make him the creative force who defined its essence as we understand it today.

Epilogue

The earliest hint we have that Peter and Paul died in the first really serious wave of anti-Christian persecution, under the Emperor Nero, comes from Pope Clement's *Letter* in the mid-90s. He records that the two apostles "who had led holy lives," were joined in their martyrdom "by a great multitude of the elect that suffered numerous indignities and tortures." Eusebius states it as fact: "It is recorded that in Nero's reign Paul was beheaded in Rome itself, and that Peter likewise was crucified and the record is confirmed by the fact that the cemeteries there are still called by the names Peter and Paul." The names of a couple of Roman cemeteries might seem a somewhat dodgy piece of evidence to rely upon for such a huge historical fact, but the church tradition behind it is very strong, and it is entirely plausible. Not long after Paul disappears from recorded history, the Christians of Rome appear center stage in the most dramatic manner imaginable.

When fire broke out in Rome on a hot July night, Nero was at his palace at Antium enjoying himself by the sea. He immediately returned to Rome and personally directed the fire-fighting operations, but to little avail. Tacitus witnessed the fire as a boy of around ten years old, and he later described the way it laid waste to Rome's palaces, temples, homes and public spaces over some nine days of continuous burning: "First, the fire swept violently over the level spaces. Then it climbed to the hills—but returned to ravage the lower ground again. It outstripped every countermeasure. The ancient city's narrow winding streets and irregular blocks encouraged its progress." His picture of what it was like for the "terrified, shrieking women, helpless young and old" who were trying to escape is vivid: "When people looked back, menacing flames sprang up before them or outflanked them. When they escaped to a neighboring quarter, the fire followed—even districts believed to be remote proved to be involved. Finally, with no idea where or what to flee, they crowded on to the country roads."

Nero's response to this crisis sounds exemplary: he threw open the Field of Mars and his own gardens for the refugees, put up emergency shelters, brought in food from Ostia and the countryside, and cut the price of corn to prevent profiteering. But the scale of the disaster—only four of Rome's fourteen districts had escaped, and Tacitus says those areas that were worst hit were "reduced to a few scorched and mangled ruins"—had created a febrile public mood, and a couple of nasty rumors started doing the rounds. It was widely believed that Nero had started the fire himself so that he could engage in grandiose rebuilding plans on the rubble. Suetonius states this as incontrovertible fact: "For under cover of displeasure at the ugliness of the old buildings and the narrow, crooked streets, he [Nero] set fire to the city so openly that several ex-consuls did not venture to lay hands on his chamberlains although they caught them on their estates with tow and firebrands." And of course there was the even more damaging whisper that has fixed an image of Nero in our minds ever since—that the emperor had enjoyed the whole thing as a spectacle, dressed up in the theatrical gear that he so loved, singing of the sack of Troy (fiddles had not been invented) as Rome's past went up in smoke before his eyes. Suetonius writes:

> Besides an immense number of dwellings, the houses of leaders of old were burned, still adorned with trophies of victory, and the temples of the gods vowed and dedicated by the kings and later in the Punic and Gallic wars, and whatever else interesting and noteworthy had survived from antiquity. Viewing the conflagration from the tower of Maecenas, and exulting, as he [Nero] said, "with the beauty of the flames," he sang the whole time the "Sack of Ilium," in his regular stage costume.

To put a stop to this kind of talk, the emperor needed a scapegoat, and he found one in Rome's Christians. There is some evidence that there was a Christian community in the area near the eastern end of the Circus Maximus where the fire started, and it is easy to see how the kind of apocalyptic teaching embraced by Pauline Christians could be used against them in these tumultuous days. "Nero fastened the guilt and inflicted the most exquisite tortures on a class hated for their abominations, called Christians by the populace," Tacitus declares. He details the punishments inflicted on the Christians in lurid terms—to say they suffered "numerous indignities and tortures" is putting it mildly. "Their execution was made a matter of sport; some were sewn up in the skins of wild beasts and savaged to death by dogs; others were fastened to crosses as living torches, to serve as lights when daylight failed." It suggests some kind of theatrical *tableau vivant*, perhaps a representation of the death of Actaeon, the mythical hunter who was torn to pieces by his own hounds. And Tacitus, who, like Suetonius, was no fan of Nero's, cannot resist a jibe at the emperor's habit of dressing up and showing off in public: "Nero made his gardens available for the show and held games in the Circus, mingling with the crowd or standing in his chariot in charioteers' uniform."

The incident provided Christianity with one of the most powerful symbolic narratives of its early history—and its immediacy was preserved with particular vividness by virtue of the fact that the Vatican was later laid out where Nero's gardens once led down to the banks of the Tiber. If either Peter or Paul were in Rome during Nero's persecution it is highly likely that they would have perished.

The great fire of Rome was in the summer of 64; Nero stabbed himself in the throat after a coup against him in June 68 (his end was suitably unpleasant; "he died," according to Suetonius, "with his eyes glazed and bulging from their sockets, a sight that horrified everybody present"). So we could advance a— very tentative—argument for placing Paul's death sometime in the mid to late 60s, around a decade after the composition of the Letter to the Romans. That could mean he lived for perhaps as much as six or seven years after his last New Testament appearance.

Tradition has it that, in contrast to his co-religionists who died such horrible deaths in Nero's spectacles, Paul was beheaded, because it was his right as a Roman citizen to die relatively painlessly. There is no independent evidence for this whatever, but there is a church on the spot where it is supposed to have happened. It contains three fountains that are said to have sprung up where his head bounced when it was severed from his body (looking at the distance of several yards that separates them, one cannot help reflecting that he must have had a very bouncy head).

But any chronology for Paul's final days is highly speculative. The theories about how long he lived and what he did after his disappearance from written history range from the scholarly to the comical, and even the most closely argued should be treated with extreme skepticism. Paul's story now becomes a little like an interactive computer game; you, the reader, can decide from a menu of options how you would like the narrative to develop.

You might wish to take the "Roman" Paul so firmly established by Luke in the final chapters of Acts to his logical conclusion, so to speak. An imaginative third-century writer tried to turn the apostle into a civilized classical rhetorician and thinker by creating a substantial correspondence between Paul and the Stoic philosopher Seneca. Seneca was Nero's tutor and adviser—he was eventually forced to take his own life when Nero turned against him. Fourteen letters are said to have been exchanged between him and the apostle, and they include an episode when Seneca reads some of Paul's thoughts to Nero himself. The sequence opens with a charming vignette of a group of philosophers strolling in a garden as they talk. "I would like you to know," reads the first of the *Letters* of Seneca, "that after reading of your booklet, that is, a number of letters that you have addressed to city churches or the chief cities of provinces and that contain wonderful exhortations for the moral life, we are thoroughly refreshed." Paul's answer has all the charm of an urbane man of letters exchanging academic courtesies with a peer: "Since you write that you were somehow agreeably touched by my letter, I consider myself honored by this judgment of a sincere man. For being the censor, philosopher, and teacher of so distinguished a prince and also at the same time of the public, you would not say that if what you say is not true. I wish you prolonged prosperity."

It is manifestly ludicrous to suggest that such cool *politesse* could come from the pen that gave us the passion of the Letter to the Romans, the vituperative power of parts of the Second Letter to the Corinthians, or the warmth of the opening verses of Paul's Letter to the Philippians. There are a few moments of real humor in the correspondence, although it is impossible to say whether they are deliberate or not; at one point Seneca sends Paul "a book on verbosity," which did make me wonder whether the whole sequence was an elaborate joke. Seneca's comments toward the end of the correspondence on Paul's apparently impending execution after the Great Fire of Rome are wonderfully insouciant: "Can you possibly think that I am not distressed and grieved that capital punishment is still visited upon you innocent persons?... Christians and Jews are—worst luck—executed as fire raisers, as commonly happens." Not quite what one would like to receive on the eve of being rent asunder by wild dogs. But no less an authority than the church father St. Jerome, author of the Vulgate Latin version of the Bible, believed the letters to be genuine, and the myth of some kind of relationship between Seneca and Paul proved extremely tenacious.

If, on the other hand, it is Paul's flair for adventure and the theatrical gesture that appeals to you, you might prefer to think of his end as it appears in *The Acts of Paul,* a collection of curious Pauline myths and legends put together by a middle-ranking church official in Asia Minor in the late second century. It includes an incident when Paul baptizes a lion near Ephesus. The lion is subsequently captured and sent to eat him by the authorities, but the two fall into amiable conversation and Paul is saved. As a mark of its newfound faith the lion exhibits an admirable capacity for sexual restraint ("The lion ran off into the countryside rejoicing.... A lioness met him, and he did not yield himself to her") and the theme of sexual continence is memorably developed in the most famous of these stories, known as the *Acts of Paul and Thecla.*

These *Acts* sometimes appear independently as a freestanding book, and they tell a morality tale of extraordinary devotion to the ideal of Christian virginity. Thecla, a young woman of Iconium, spent three days sitting discreetly at a window, listening to Paul preach, and admiring the many "women and virgins" going in to see the great man in the flesh. So impressed was she by his praise for the chaste life that she rejected her fiancé and dedicated herself to following the apostle. This was apparently a very shocking step in Iconium society, and Thecla's own mother urges that she be burnt at the stake *"pour encourager les autres"*—Paul was evidently having some success among the maidens of the city. But God sends a hailstorm to quench the flames and Thecla is saved. Paul then took her with him to Antioch (it is not clear which one), where a rich Syrian was overcome with lust at the sight of her and tried to force himself upon her in the street. She fought him off, again insisting on her virtue, and he was so angry that he arranged for her to be thrown to the wild beasts. Again God protects her; she was tied to a lioness but it simply licked her feet, and the various hungry bears and raging bulls sent to finish her off were all driven back by one form of divine intervention or another.

Paul's role in Thecla's story is somewhat ambiguous. Although full of praise for her strength of will, he keeps abandoning her at critical moments, and because he refuses to baptize her she is forced to baptize herself in a pit full of water and man-eating seals in the arena while she is fighting off the assorted bears, bulls, and lions. But once he reaches Rome, Paul is heroically brave himself. Unlike the Acts of the Apostles, *The Acts of Paul* gives us a gratifyingly dramatic confrontation between Paul and Nero. The emperor accuses him of slipping into his dominions and enlisting soldiers of "the great King [Christ]," to which Paul defiantly replies, "Caesar, not only from thy province do we enlist soldiers, but from the whole world." He is duly beheaded, and "when the executioner struck off his head, milk spurted upon the soldier's clothing." This version of the story ends with Paul making a triumphant resurrection appearance and really intimidating Nero:

> Then Paul came about the ninth hour, when many philosophers and the centurion were standing with Caesar, and he stood before them all and said, "Caesar, here I am—Paul, God's soldier. I am not dead, but alive in God. But for thee, unhappy man, there shall be many

evils and great punishment, because thou didst unjustly shed the blood of the righteous, and that not many days hence!"

The church historian Tertullian dismissed *The Acts of Paul* as a fraud in the early third century, but some of these stories were still being written about seriously in Christian literature right up until the late Middle Ages.

Those with a nose for an academic detective story can follow the school that gives Paul a whole new lease of life after the end of the Acts of the Apostles. It springs from a very respectable scholarly tradition, which begins with that brief passage about Paul in Pope Clement's late first-century *Letter to the Corinthians:*

> Through jealousy and strife Paul demonstrated how to win the prize of patient endurance: seven times he was imprisoned; he was forced to leave and stoned; he preached in the East and the West; and, finally, he won the splendid renown that his faith had earned. He taught the right manner of life to the whole world, traveled as far as the western boundary, and, when he had given testimony before the authorities, ended his earthly career and was taken up into the holy place as the greatest model of patient endurance.

The "western boundary" is sometimes translated as "the extremity of the west" or the "boundary of the setting sun," and is generally taken to be a reference to Spain. It is not surprising that people have put this together with the plan to travel to Spain outlined in the Letter to the Romans and concluded that Paul did indeed make it to Rome's most western province. Jerome Murphy O'Connor concludes that the reason we do not know about Paul's Spanish mission is that it proved a failure, largely because of a language barrier. He gives Paul a summer in Spain and then dispatches him round the Aegean one final time before sending him back to Rome to face his martyrdom. Other accounts put Gaul and Crete as well as Spain on the list of countries Paul visited during his final years. The kindly Abbot Dom Paolo at St.

Paul's Outside the Walls even suggested Paul visited America, although on what basis I cannot possibly imagine.

Those who follow this school tend to argue for the authenticity of the Second Letter to Timothy, one of those pastoral letters that are more generally judged to be too distinctive to merit a place in the true canon of Paul's letters. They do so partly on the basis of the very personal nature of some passages in the letter: "When you come," the author says, "bring the cloak that I left with Carpus at Troas, also the books, and above all the parchments" (2 Tim 4:13). What on earth would be the point of this, the argument runs, if the pastoral letters were forgeries designed to deal with problems in church management several years after Paul's death? If one allows for the possibility that the letter is genuine it does paint a most affecting picture of Paul in his final days. He sends it, so the theory goes, during his second imprisonment in Rome, where he has returned after his trip to Spain and his final journey around the eastern Mediterranean. He has been abandoned by most of his friends: "Do your best to come to me soon," he writes to Timothy, "for Demas, in love with this present world, has deserted me and gone to Thessalonica; Crescens has gone to Galatia, Titus to Dalmatia. Only Luke is with me" (2 Tim 4:9–11). And one of the letter's best-known passages reflects a powerful sense of foreboding:

> As for me, I am already being poured out as a libation, and the time of my departure has come. I have fought the good fight, I have finished the race, I have kept the faith. From now on there is reserved for me the crown of righteousness, which the Lord, the righteous judge, will give to me on that day, and not only to me but also to all who have longed for his appearing. (2 Tim 4:6–8)

However, once you have sent Paul wandering off on his missionary journeys again, you can—if you are so tempted—reopen the whole question of where he actually died. The way the paragraph from Pope Clement that I have quoted above is phrased has led some to conclude that Paul was in fact martyred during his trip to Spain. There is an even odder tradition that has him buried—if not necessarily martyred—back on his old stomping ground of Philippi. The archaeologist in charge of excavations there, Samuel Provost, has become increasingly intrigued by the evidence that in the early Christian era several basilicas were built in the city; his team have found traces of five already, and when I toured the site with him he was hinting excitedly at the possibility of a sixth—far more than were needed to serve the needs of the population. The area covered by Philippi was, by the standards of a modern city, really quite modest, and the basilicas were absolutely huge; if you imagine a small English country town that contained Westminster Abbey, York Minster, a couple of Durham Cathedrals, and St. Paul's in London thrown in for good measure, you get an idea of what Philippi must once have looked like.

The one obvious explanation is that the city was a destination for pilgrims, and there's a clue to the attraction that might have brought them there in a marble sarcophagus found near the center of the city. It is in a prominent place in a church that is thought to have been associated with the cult of a saint—the design is consistent with other churches known for such cults—and it is thought likely that the sarcophagus would have contained the relics of the saint in question. There is a curious piece of guttering emerging from the side of the sarcophagus, and the theory is that water would have been poured into the top, passing over the saint's bones and emerging from the guttering to be collected by the pilgrims, rather as water from the spring at Lourdes is sold in bottles to pilgrims today. There is absolutely no hard evidence that the saint whose bones lay here was St. Paul, but even Dr. Provost, who to me seemed dauntingly rigorous in his scientific approach to his work, could not help musing, "You must recognize that it is a bit weird not to have any hard evidence about Paul in Rome.... I mean, you have to admit it is a bit strange."

The end you choose for Paul will almost certainly be influenced by whether you like and admire him. That early fan, St. John Chrysostom, places the apostle's martyrdom firmly in Rome, and gives it a twist of his own. He has Paul converting a beautiful concubine belonging to Nero, and relates that the emperor took his revenge in a fit of jealous rage. Chrysostom's reflections on the final confrontation between Nero and Paul—

which he is clearly convinced took place—allow him to develop an eloquent and improving homily around the question, "Would you be on the side of Nero, or Paul?" Not for nothing was this St. John known as "the golden tongued." He paints a shining picture of Nero's greatness; he was

> a tyrant, had obtained great success, had raised many trophies, had wealth ever flowing in, numerous armies everywhere; he had the greater part of the world and the imperial city subject to his sway, the whole senate crouching to him, and his palace, too, was advancing with splendid show. When he must be armed, he went forth arrayed in gold and precious stones. When he was to sit in peace, he sat clothed in robes of purple.
>
> [Paul, by contrast,] was a man who often lived in hunger, often went to bed without food, a man who was naked, and had not clothes to put on; "in cold, and nakedness," as he says of himself. Nor was this all; but he was cast into prison at the command of Nero himself, and confined with robbers, with impostors, with grave breakers, with murderers, and he was, as he himself says, scourged as a malefactor.

You have probably guessed roughly where all this is leading by now: "The one said, 'Do not disseminate the word of God.' The other said, 'I cannot forbear, the word of God is not bound.' Thus the Cilician, the prisoner, the poor tentmaker, who lived in hunger, despised the Roman, rich as he was, and emperor, and ruling over all...."

For past generations much of Paul's allure lay in the fact that he was such a wonderful hook on which to hang all kinds of Christian ornaments—moral teachings, myths and legends, powerful symbols, dogmas and doctrines. For today's generation the appeal is almost the reverse: it is the fact that he is so human and so real, so anchored in history; we can read the words he wrote for ourselves and match the stories of his life against our growing understanding of antiquity. For our intellectual ancestors Paul was a spur to the imagination and an inspiration for creative religious thought; they took him as a starting point and allowed their minds to open up all sorts of rich—and sometimes dangerous—fields of religious endeavor and exploration. My journey has been in the opposite direction; I have tried to work my way back through the thickets of religious history and interpretation to the irreducible core of the man himself.

Of course I would not claim to have found it, but the journey has been rewarding rather in the way of those precious occasions that really make journalism worthwhile—when you meet a truly remarkable person and, even just for a moment or two, get a glimmer of an insight into what drives them. I am perfectly sure I have been guilty of the historical sin I have accused so many others of committing, and that my Paul is very much the Paul of my own prejudices; this version of the apostle belongs to the twenty-first century as surely as Sir William Ramsey's does to the nineteenth, and St. John Chrysostom's to the fourth. Perhaps it is precisely because Paul remains an enigma, resisting our best efforts to pin him down, that he will always intrigue us, and each new generation will reinvent him.

Chronology

There is one point of Pauline chronology on which all modern scholars agree—that Paul was in Corinth while Gallio, brother of the Roman philosopher Seneca, was governor of the province of Achaia. The Acts of the Apostles refers to Paul being brought before a certain "Gallio" in Corinth (Acts 18:12), but the significance of this reference did not become apparent until the discovery of the Delphi inscription I have referred to in chapter 9. Although some fragments of the inscription were found in 1905 it took some time for the other bits and pieces that give us our understanding of it to turn up, and it was not until 1970 that they were published in the full form we have today. What has emerged is a letter from the emperor Claudius that mentions "L. Junius Gallio, my friend and proconsul." The exact date of Gallio's arrival in Achaia and the duration of his governorship remain uncertain, so even this encouragingly independent corroboration of St. Luke's account does not give us a precise chronological linchpin to work around. However, it is generally accepted that Paul's encounter with Gallio took place between AD 50 and 52, and most modern chronologies of Paul's life take that as a starting point.

Almost everything else is disputed, often hotly and always with a great weight of scholarship being brought to bear on the argument. What follows does not make any claim to be definitive—it is intended only to be a helpful skeleton on which to hang the story I have tried to flesh out in this book. Even though the dates are very uncertain, the sequence in which I have placed events seems to me to offer the best way of making sense of what we know of Paul's life. However, I am very conscious that several

Pauline experts who have spent much longer trying to piece this jigsaw together than I could ever do take a different view—many, for example, place the Jerusalem Council much later in Paul's career, and there are still some who judge the Letter to the Galatians to be the apostle's first.

AD

1–10   Paul is born in Tarsus.

30   Jesus is crucified in Jerusalem.

32   The stoning of Stephen takes place during Paul's time as a persecutor of Christians.

33 or 34 Paul has his conversion experience in Damascus.

34–42   These are the "lost" years during which Paul travels in "Arabia," spends some time in his home city of Tarsus, and briefly visits the apostles in Jerusalem.

43 or 44 Barnabas summons Paul to Antioch, where he spends two years working with the city's Christians.

45–48   Paul makes his first missionary journey with Barnabas, traveling to Cyprus and Asia Minor.

48 or 49 Paul meets James, Peter, and the rest of the Jerusalem church at the Jerusalem Council.

49–52   Paul makes his second missionary journey, crossing to Europe for the first time and spending eighteen months in Corinth, where he writes the first of his letters, to the Thessalonians.

52   Paul appears before the proconsul Gallio in Corinth.

52–55	Paul settles in Ephesus on his third missionary journey. While he is there he writes his Letter to the Galatians, and the letter we know as 1 Corinthians. He sends Timothy to act as his envoy in Corinth, and perhaps pays a brief visit to the city himself.
55	Paul spends some time in prison in Ephesus, and writes to his friend Philemon and to the Christians of Philippi. On his release he leaves Ephesus for Macedonia. He writes the Second Letter to the Corinthians on the road.
55–56	Paul winters in Corinth, where he writes his Letter to the Romans.
56	Paul travels to Jerusalem with his offering for the church there, and is jailed by the Roman authorities.
56–58	Paul is held in Caesarea.
59	Paul is taken to Rome.
mid-60s	Martyrdom.

Bibliography

Much of the material for this book was drawn from interviews conducted for the BBC Radio Four Series *In the Footsteps of St. Paul*—transcripts of the six programs in the series were placed on the BBC Web site at www.bbc.co.uk/religion. All scriptural quotations are taken from the New Revised Standard Version of the Bible. Those books I have quoted or made reference to in the text are listed below, together with one or two others I have found especially helpful for background information and ideas.

Arnold, Matthew, *Complete Prose Works* (Ann Arbor, MI, 1965).

Belloc, Hilaire, *Europe and the Faith* (Tan Books, Rockford, IL, 1992).

Cicero, Marcus Tullius, *Orations,* tr. C. D. Yonge (Henry G. Bohn, London, 1851).

Cimok, Fatih, *Saint Paul in Anatolia* (A Turizm Yayinlari, 2001).

Chrysostom, St. John, *Homilies* (John Henry Parker, Oxford, 1852).

Deissmann, Adolf, *St. Paul: A Study in Social and Religious History* (Hodder and Stoughton, 1912).

Deleanu, Daniel, *The Islamic Jesus: The Portrait of Jesus in Islamic Literature and Tradition* (Writers Club Press, 2002).

Den Heyer, C. J., *Paul: A Man of Two Worlds* (SCM Press, London, 2000).

Eusebius, bishop of Caesarea, *Ecclesiastical History,* tr. H. Lawlor and J. Oulton (Society for Promoting Christian Knowledge, 1927).

Friedlander, Ludwig, *Roman Life and Manners Under the Early Empire,* tr. J. Freese and Leonard Magnus (Routledge & Kegan Paul, 1965).

Golomb, Jacob, and Robert Wistrich, *Nietzsche: Godfather of Fascism? On the Uses and Abuses of Philosophy* (Princeton University Press, 2002).

Gore, Charles, *St. Paul's Epistle to the Romans: A Practical Exposition* (John Murray, London, 1901).

Harman Akenson, Donald, *Saint Saul: A Skeleton Key to the Historical Jesus* (Oxford University Press, 2000).

Hennecke, E. and W. Schneemelcher, *New Testament Apocrypha* (2 vols.), tr. R. McL.Wilson (Lutterworth, London, 1963).

Hitler, *Table Talk,* tr. Norman Cameron and R. H. Stevens (Weidenfeld and Nicholson, 1953).

Johnson, Paul, *A History of the Jews* (Phoenix Press, London, 1995).

Josephus, Flavius, *Works,* tr. William Whiston (William Allason, London, 1818).

Kleist, James, *The Epistles of St. Clement of Rome and St. Ignatius of Antioch* (Longmans, Green & Co., London, 1946).

Libanius, *Antioch as a Centre of Hellenic Culture,* tr. A. F. Norman (Liverpool University Press, 2000).

Luther, Martin, *Works* (Concordia Publishing, St. Louis, MO, 1958).

Maccoby, Hyman, *The Mythmaker: St. Paul and the Invention of Christianity* (Barnes & Noble, New York, 1998).

Maqsood, Ruqaiyyah Waris, *The Mysteries of Jesus* (Sakina Books, Oxford, 2000).

Meeks, Wayne, *The First Urban Christians: The Social World of the Apostle Paul* (Yale University Press, New Haven, CT, 2003).

Morton, H. V., *In the Steps of St. Paul* (Methuen, 2002).

Mount, Christopher, *Pauline Christianity: Luke-Acts and the Legacy of Paul,* Supplements to *Novum Testamentum* (Brill, 2002).

Murphy O'Connor, Jerome, *Paul: A Critical Life* (Clarendon Press, Oxford, 1996).

Nietzsche, Friedrich, *Twilight of the Idols: The Anti-Christ,* tr. R. J. Hollingdale (Penguin, 1968).

Philostratus, Flavius, *The Life of Apollonius of Tyana,* tr. J. S. Phillimore (Clarendon Press, Oxford, 1946).

Ramsay, W. M., *St. Paul the Traveller and Roman Citizen* (Hodder & Stoughton, 1895).

Robertson, F. W., *Expository Lectures on St. Paul's Epistle to the Corinthians* (Smith, Elder & Co, London, 1865).

Roetzel, Calvin, *Paul: The Man and the Myth* (T and T Clark, Edinburgh, 1999).

Sanders, E. P., *Paul: A Very Short Introduction* (Oxford University Press, 1991).

Schweitzer, Albert, *Paul and His Interpreters: A Critical History* (A & C Black, London, 1912).

Schweitzer, Albert, *The Mysticism of Paul the Apostle* (A & C Black, London, 1931).

Schonfield, Hugh, J., *The Jew of Tarsus: An Unorthodox Portrait of Paul* (Macdonald & Co., London, 1946).

Smallwood, Edith Mary, *The Jews Under Roman Rule: From Pompey to Diocletian* (Brill, 1976)

Smith, David, *The Life and Letters of St. Paul* (Hodder & Stoughton, 1919).

Bibliography

Smith, James, *The Voyage and Shipwreck of St. Paul* (Longman, Brown, Green, 1848).

Strabo, *The Geography,* tr. Horace Jones (William Heinemann, London, 1928).

Suetonius, *Lives of 12 Caesars,* tr. Alexander Thomson (Henry Bohm, London, 1855).

Tacitus, *Annals,* tr. Church and Brodribb (Macmillan, London, 1881).

Thrall, Margaret E., *The First and Second Letters to the Corinthians* (Cambridge University Press, 1965).

Wagner, J. Ross, *Heralds of Good News: Isaiah and Paul (in Concert) in the Letter to the Romans,* Supplements to *Novum Testamentum* (Brill, 2002).

Warner, Marina, *Signs and Wonders: Essays on Literature and Culture* (Chatto and Windus, London, 2003).

Wiles, Maurice F., *The Divine Apostle* (Cambridge University Press, 1967).

Wilson, A. N., *Paul: The Mind of the Apostle* (Sinclair-Stevenson, 1997).

Wright, Tom, *What Saint Paul Really Said* (Lion, Oxford, 1997).

General Index

Index of Bible Verses Cited

The books are listed in biblical order.